GLORIOUS!

THE ST. LOUIS BLUES' HISTORIC QUEST FOR THE 2019 STANLEY CUP

This book is available in quantity at special discounts for your group or organization.
For further information, contact:

Triumph Books LLC
814 North Franklin Street
Chicago, Illinois 60610
Phone: (312) 337-0747
www.triumphbooks.com

Printed in U.S.A.
ISBN: 978-1-62937-665-3

St. Louis Post-Dispatch
Roger Hensley, Assistant Managing Editor-Sports
Mike Smith, Online Sports Editor
Gary Hairlson, Multimedia Director

Content packaged by Mojo Media, Inc.
Joe Funk: Editor
Jason Hinman: Creative Director

Front and back cover photos by Laurie Skrivan/St. Louis Post-Dispatch

PHOTOGRAPHERS
St. Louis Post-Dispatch
David Carson: 45, 54; Robert Cohen: 105, 106; J.B. Forbes: 3, 4, 9, 11, 12, 15, 25, 27. 29. 36, 48, 49, 52, 62, 75, 77, 83, 84, 87, 89, 91, 93, 95, 97, 99, 101, 102, 109, 111, 112, 115; Benjamin Hochman: 56; Chris Lee: 32, 58; Colter Peterson: 35, 38, 40, 42, 46, 117, 118, 121, 122, 125, 126, 128; Laurie Skrivan: 1, 6, 17, 19, 21, 23, 30-31
Additional Photos by AP Images: 51, 60, 67, 68, 71, 72, 79, 80

CONTENTS

INTRODUCTION

52-YEAR QUEST FOR ST. LOUIS BLUES COMES TO A GLORIOUS CLOSE WITH STANLEY CUP CHAMPIONSHIP

BY JEFF GORDON

Back in the St. Louis Blues' earliest days, their fans must have believed a Stanley Cup parade was inevitable.

After all, the Blues emerged as the best of the NHL's first six expansion franchises. They played for the Cup in 1968, 1969 and 1970, losing to Montreal twice and Boston once. Those early teams set an aggressive tone that carried throughout the franchise's history.

But the wait for the Cup became excruciating. Decade after decade passed without a championship. And then came an epic title run that finally occurred — in the spring of 2019 — when fans least expected it.

General manager Doug Armstrong fired coach Mike Yeo on Nov. 19, 2018 and promoted assistant coach Craig Berube to replace him on an interim basis. Berube set out to clean up the team's defensive play, build team cohesion and rebuild the group's confidence.

Change did not come easily or quickly. The Blues sat dead last in the NHL on Jan. 3, 2019. Armstrong wondered if the roster needed a makeover. Rival general managers were inquiring about all of his key players.

The Blues faced a brutal schedule during the second half of the season, 25 of 41 games on the road. But that challenge became their blessing, since the players bonded on the road and started playing for each other.

"We did a good job of sticking together and coming together," Blues winger Jaden Schwartz recalled. "We just couldn't seem to put three or four wins together. We'd beat a really good team, we'd lose. We'd win, we'd lose. We just couldn't put together a streak. Then finally we pulled it together. We never really had that mindset where we were completely out of it, but we knew that we were running out of time and we kind of just got our mojo as a team."

With rookie Jordan Binnington rising from obscurity to catch fire in goal, the Blues reversed course with an 11-game winning streak. They climbed up the standings and into the playoff bracket.

The Blues upset the Winnipeg Jets in the first round, outlasted the Dallas Stars in the second round, hammered the San Jose Sharks in the Western Conference finals and then stopped the streaking Boston Bruins to win the Cup.

That was only fitting, since the Bruins beat the Blues the last time they played for the Cup. Bob Plager was on the ice for the Blues back in 1970, and he was still with the franchise when it finally claimed hockey's biggest prize.

"In St. Louis, you walk around there, and every time you talk to somebody about the Blues, it's 'we.' It's their team," Plager said. "They've been waiting a long time, and they deserve it. I mean, they've been great fans. I've always said, I'd love to win the Stanley Cup. The players would. But we owe it to the fans, the people."

Many ownership groups came and went as the franchise teetered on thin financial ice. That has been a persistent story line.

But the other recurring Blues theme has been outsized ambition.

The franchise launched the Hall of Fame coaching career of Scotty Bowman during its expansion era and employed many prominent veterans, including Glenn Hall, Jacques Plante, Red Berenson, Al Arbour, Dickie Moore, Doug Harvey, Ab McDonald, Frank St. Marseille, Phil Goyette and, of course, Barclay and Bob Plager.

"There was nothing more unfair than expansion," Hall observed. "The existing teams kept all the players. The expansion teams were left with the guys they thought were over the hill. The league was very lucky St. Louis represented the expansion teams very well or the league might have gone belly up."

Emile "The Cat" Francis drove the next big push, starting with the 1976 draft that landed forwards Bernie Federko and Brian Sutter plus goaltender Mike Liut. Under Ralston Purina's

Coach Craig Berube hugs Blues legend Bob Plager after the Game 7 victory in the Stanley Cub Final.

ownership, Francis had the resources to load up. By 1980-81 the Blues had a 107-point squad featuring three strong scoring lines. While that team went nowhere in the playoffs, it was arguably the most talented squad the franchise ever assembled.

"That was a very exciting time for me," Francis later said. "There we were, on the brink of extinction, then to come all the way back like we did and get the support that we needed … that was like a dream come true."

The dream did not last. After R. Hal Dean left his lead role with Ralston Purina, the company wanted out of hockey. It found a buyer in Saskatoon, Saskatchewan, but the NHL nixed the sale in 1983. Harry Ornest swooped in from Beverly Hills, Calif., bought the franchise, put Jack Quinn in charge of the business and Ron Caron in charge of the hockey operation.

Caron hired the right coach, Jacques Demers, and made heady trades that landed Mark Hunter, Greg Paslawski and Doug Wickenheiser among others. Despite trading away pricey veterans Liut and forward Joe Mullen on orders from Ornest, the frenetic Caron assembled a team that reached the 1986 Western Conference Final. The Blues famously rallied in the "Monday Night Miracle" in Game 6 before falling to Calgary in Game 7.

Caron went along for the ride as Blues chairman Mike Shanahan and team president Quinn turned the franchise into the NHL's renegade operation. They tried to surround emerging superstar Brett Hull with as much star power as possible.

"Hull played a role in people realizing there was hockey in the United States outside of Chicago," Shanahan said. "My theory of sports is that people want to see stars play. It's the entertainment business and it's built around stars, and Brett Hull was the brightest star."

No team dared to sign free agents back then, but the Blues did — plucking Scott Stevens from the Washington Capitals in 1990 at the cost of five first-round draft picks.

When the Blues tried their next big play, signing New Jersey Devils free agent Brendan Shanahan in 1991, the league was ready to strike back. The collective bargaining agreement called for an arbitrator to resolve compensation for a free agent signing and Judge Edward Houston famously awarded Stevens to the Devils. Ouch!

Judge Houston's harsh rebuke only made the Blues more aggressive. They landed elite offensive defenseman Phil Housley in 1993 and, when that didn't pay off big, they flipped him for Al MacInnis a year later.

The franchise stunningly hired Cup-winning coach Mike Keenan as coach and general manager in 1994, even though he was still under contract with the New York Rangers for four more years. Such trifling details were of no concern to Blues management.

That was the ultimate outlaw play and it led to a steady barrage of player moves. Iron Mike acquired many of his former players along with an army of former Edmonton Oilers (including Wayne Gretzky and Grant Fuhr) and some quality veterans (including Chris Pronger and Dale Hawerchuk) while trying to duplicate his success in New York.

But Keenan didn't have Mark Messier on his team, as he did with the Rangers, so he failed to bring the Cup to St. Louis.

(Long after that renegade regime was gone, the NHL punished the Blues for vindictive tampering with Scott Stevens when he was due a new deal in New Jersey. That "abhorrent" conduct, as commissioner Gary Bettman put it, cost the club $1.4 million and a first-round pick.)

The next big push came after Bill and Nancy Laurie poured their Walmart billions into the franchise in 1999. Once again the Blues targeted big-name talent and built unrealistically large payrolls, landing cornerstone forwards Keith Tkachuk and Doug Weight, among others.

The Blues reached one Final Four in that era — in 2001, with Joel Quenneville behind the bench and Pronger and MacInnis patrolling the blue line — and they made three more playoff trips before the Lauries ordered a fire sale as they fled the pro sports business.

The franchise rebuilt during the Dave Checketts Era and gradually regained its competitive standing. Then Tom Stillman's ownership group stepped in and raised the bar, spending to the NHL's salary cap again and again to improve the team.

The Blues advanced to the playoffs seven times in the past eight years, reaching the Final Four in 2016 under coach Ken Hitchcock but losing to the Sharks in the Western Conference Final.

Then the franchise began the retooling to construct the franchise's first Cup-winning team. Armstrong's "all in" bid for the 2018-19 season — trading for Ryan O'Reilly and signing free agents David Perron, Tyler Bozak and Pat Maroon in the summer of '18 — finally put the Blues over the top.

"We have two overriding goals: No. 1, win the Stanley Cup; it's time to do that," Stillman said after becoming majority owner in 2012. "The second is to make sure the Blues franchise is stable and sustainable here in St. Louis for years to come. No. 1 would help with No. 2."

Mission accomplished. Finally. ■

Captain Alex Pietrangelo lifts the Stanley Cup for the first time in St. Louis Blues history.

BRUINS 4, BLUES 2
MAY 27, 2019 • BOSTON, MASSACHUSETTS

BEANTOWN MELTDOWN

DESPITE SURGING AHEAD, BLUES STILL CAN'T WIN IN STANLEY CUP FINAL

BY JIM THOMAS

It now is 51 years and counting, but the Blues still haven't won a game in the Stanley Cup Final.

They were swept in four games in their three previous Cup Final appearances — in 1968 and 1969 against the Montreal Canadiens and in 1970 against the Boston Bruins.

On Monday night it was same story, different century.

The Blues looked good early, jumping to a 2-0 lead early in the second period. But with towel-waving Robert Kraft, owner of football's New England Patriots in the house, Boston stormed back for a 4-2 victory at TD Garden in Game 1 of the best-of-seven series.

It was the Bruins' eighth straight victory in these playoffs — they have outscored their opponents 32-11 in that stretch. And it ran their postseason record to 9-0 against the Blues, including a 4-0 sweep in the 1970 Stanley Cup Final, the last time the Blues were in the title round.

"We've been real disciplined most of the playoffs pretty much," coach Craig Berube said. "We weren't tonight obviously with five penalties. We gotta be better there."

Entering Monday's contest, the Blues were the least-penalized team in the playoffs this season, spending an average of 6.18 minutes in the penalty box per game. That wasn't the case Monday, when they were whistled for five penalties compared to two for Boston.

"I'm not gonna judge the calls, but they did happen," the Blues' David Perron said. "We were in the box too much and that gave them the chance to get their touches and kinda get going in their game and shoot pucks on net.

"The number (of shots) looked bad and a lot of it happened on the power play. And we just didn't play good enough in the second."

No they didn't. After taking a 2-0 lead one minute into the second period on Vladimir Tarasenko's ninth goal of the playoffs, it was all Boston.

Connor Clifton got behind the Blues' defense for a tap-in goal on a pinpoint pass from Sean Kuraly 76 seconds after Tarasenko's goal. Clifton beat his former teammate from the Providence Bruins, goalie Jordan Binnington, on the play.

Charlie McAvoy scored on the power play with 7:19 left in the period to tie the game at 2-2. And then Kuraly got the winner 5:21 into the third period, getting the puck past Joel Edmundson and then Binnington during a scramble in front of the net.

The Blues were outshot 18-3 in the second period and 30-12 over the final two periods.

"It's just a reflection of we didn't have the puck down low," the Blues' Jay Bouwmeester said. "We just played into their hands. It's tough to win when you take five penalties, especially against a team that has a real good power play."

It took several scrambling saves and spectacular saves by Binnington to keep the Blues in it before Brad Marchand scored an empty-net goal with 1:49 left.

"When that first goal went in they got some momentum, and then a big push there," said Binnington, who made 34 saves. "You could feel them coming and they were coming hard and the rink was buzzing."

In comparison, the Blues mustered only 20 shots and went the last 11:44 of the second and the first 4:33 of the third without a shot on goal — a total drought of 16:17.

"I think we're fine in here," Perron said. "We know what we did is we went to the box too much. We lost our composure a little bit. We were not getting to our game enough below the goal line, things like that.

"But I think we're gonna be a lot better next game."

The Bruins entered the game with a scalding 34 percent success rate on the power play in the postseason, so the Blues were playing into their hands by sending out the Boston power play so many times. And the Blues weren't always happy about the calls.

Edmundson was sent off for high-sticking former Blues

The Blues and Bruins converge after Blues goalie Jordan Binnington lost sight of the puck between his legs during the first period of the Game 1 loss.

captain David Backes 5½ minutes into the second period.

Edmundson reacted as if he thought Backes was guilty of embellishment, and gave a shove to Backes in the back while the Boston forward was on the ice.

The Blues killed that one off. They weren't as fortunate 5½ minutes later when Oskar Sundqvist was sent off for hooking, at the 11:04 mark of the second. Sundqvist complained about that call as well, drawing boos from the crowd at TD Garden. That penalty led to the game-tying goal by McAvoy.

"Yeah, I mean there's a couple where we weren't sure," Perron said. "But it is what it is. . . . It's a fast game out there and we just gotta make sure our sticks aren't in there. Same with my penalty."

This is Boston's 20th Stanley Cup Final and Monday marked its first victory in those 20 when trailing by two or more goals.

But it was more than the penalties that stymied St. Louis.

The Blues just couldn't generate anything for most of the final two periods, as a quick, aggressive Boston squad kept the Blues bottled up in their own zone much of the time.

"They pressure you. They come hard," Berube said. "They're a quick team. They get on you. They've got good sticks. They do a lot of good things. ... They force you into bad situations with the puck a lot of times."

And in terms of physical play, they matched the Blues hit by hit. By game's end Boston had 32 hits to the Blues' 33. A hit by Torey Krug leveled Robert Thomas midway through the third period and the Blues' rookie did not return. ■

STANLEY CUP FINAL, GAME 2

BLUES 3, BRUINS 2 (OT)
MAY 29, 2019 • BOSTON, MASSACHUSETTS

FINALS FIRST

GUNNARSSON'S OT GOAL DELIVERS FIRST TITLE-SERIES VICTORY IN BLUES HISTORY

BY JIM THOMAS

Some call him Boom-Boom, because he doesn't exactly have the hardest shot around.

"Tonight it was hard, so I'm happy about that," said teammate and fellow Swede Oskar Sundqvist.

Defenseman Carl Gunnarsson had more than enough "boom" to silence TD Garden and give the Blues their first victory in a Stanley Cup Final in franchise history.

His goal with 3 minutes 51 seconds gone in overtime gave the Blues a 3-2 victory over the Boston Bruins and sent the best-of-seven series back to St. Louis tied 1-1.

"He's been around for a long time," Joel Edmundson said. "I think that was the biggest goal of his career and it couldn't have come at a better time."

Mere minutes after the dramatic game-winner, the story behind the story leaked out.

"Craig (Berube) said that he met him at the (urinal) after the third period," Sundqvist said. "And Gunny said all I need is one more chance. So it worked out."

That it did. With just 1:57 left in regulation, Gunnarsson's shot hit the corner of the net where the post and the crossbar meet. It came oh-so-close to going in.

He made amends in overtime, shooting a one-timer from just inside the blueline through traffic and past Boston goalie Tuukka Rask. It was Gunnarsson's first goal in 56 career playoff games.

And in this memorable Blues playoff run, it ranks right up there with Jaden Schwartz's "lucky pinball" (as Winnipeg goalie Connor Hellebuyck called it) with 15 seconds left to win Game 5 against the Jets. Or Pat Maroon's double-overtime Game 7 winner against Dallas. And Robert Bortuzzo's game-winning backhand in Game 3 against San Jose.

Gunnarsson, by the way, confirmed the "restroom" conversation with Berube.

"I can't deny that," Gunnarsson said. "That's where it happened. That makes it even more fun I guess. It's a good story.

"I was close in the third with the post and I had a little talk in the locker room between periods there — before the OT — and I just told him I needed one more," Gunnarsson said.

The Blues bounced back from 1-0 and 2-1 deficits to tie the game at 2-2 on goals by first Bortuzzo and then Vladimir Tarasenko. That all happened in the first period, and that was all the scoring until Gunnarsson's game-winner — which came as Boston was about to be called for tripping Alexander Steen on his way to the net.

Ryan O'Reilly, who came on the ice after goalie Jordan Binnington left on the delayed penalty, got the primary assist.

The Blues controlled most of the third period, wearing down the Bruins with a season-high 50 hits. Boston also got worn down on the back end, playing two periods-plus with only five defensemen after Matt Grzelcyk was injured after absorbing a check from Sundqvist along the boards with 2:03 left in the first.

According to Bruins coach Bruce Cassidy, Grzelcyk was sent to the hospital for tests and evaluation. Sundqvist was penalized for cross-checking on the play and declined to comment on the hit after the game.

But David Backes, the former Blues captain and current Bruin, wasn't shy about offering his opinion.

"I don't think that's a hit we want in our game," Backes said. "It's from behind, elevated, into his head, into the glass. If that's a two-minute penalty, I think there's going to be a shortage of defensemen in this series by the end of it.

"That's in somebody else's hands. That's something I think if I'm making that hit, I'm probably watching from the bleachers for a few (games), but we'll see what happens with their player."

The Blues' Oskar Sundqvist checks the Bruins' Matt Grzelcyk into the boards during the first period of Game 2 of the Stanley Cup Final. Grzelcyk left the game injured and Sundqvist received a game suspension for the hit.

It was one of five penalties called against the Blues in the game. They have been in the box 10 times so far in this series to five for the Bruins. But the Blues overcame that. They overcame the early Boston goals by Charlie Coyle and Joakim Nordstrom, and they came out breathing fire in the overtime session, controlling the puck for much of sudden death.

"We still had energy," Edmundson said. "Our team did a good job of wearing them down throughout the 60 minutes (of regulation). We knew we had more energy than them going into the overtime, so we just laid it all on the line and we stuck to our game plan."

So the bounce-back Blues struck again Wednesday. Their Stanley Cup Final demise, roundly predicted as near certainty in some corners, was put on hold. The Blues have taken away home ice advantage from the Bruins.

When informed Tuesday that Game 1 losers end up losing the Cup Final series 77 percent of the time, Tarasenko told reporters: "This is on your side to tell some cool stats and everything else. But that's not in our heads."

Well, here's another cool stat to put in your head. Or not.

Teams winning Game 2 have gone on to win the Cup 74.7 percent of the time since 1939 (when the best-of-seven format was introduced).

So as Blues fans step back from the ledge once again, the Blues head home with momentum.

"It's a great sports fanbase and a great sports city," said Binnington, who stopped 21 of 23 shots. "They deserve it. We're happy to play for them and we're having fun doing it, playing together. We're happy to go home and perform in front of them with them on our side."

St. Louis was 0-13 in Cup Final games until Wednesday. They also were 0-9 all-time against the Bruins in the playoffs, dating back to that four-game Boston sweep in the 1970 Stanley Cup and had been outscored 52-17 in those games.

"It's great. We're not done yet, but it's obviously pretty cool," Edmundson said. "We just excited to go back to St. Louis with a 1-1 split."

They won without rookie Robert Thomas, scratched from the lineup with what's believed to be a wrist injury. Coach Craig Berube said after the morning skate that Thomas' absence was not related to the monster hit he absorbed from Torey Krug in Game 1. ◾

Carl Gunnarsson's shot gets past Bruins goalie Tuukka Rask in overtime of Game 2, giving the Blues their first Stanley Cup win in franchise history. It was also Gunnarsson's first goal in 56 career playoff games.

BRUINS 7, BLUES 2
JUNE 1, 2019 • ST. LOUIS, MISSOURI

FROM FRENZY TO FRUSTRATION

BLUES FALL FLAT IN FIRST STANLEY CUP FINAL GAME IN ST. LOUIS SINCE 1970

BY JIM THOMAS

Some 17,924 days ago, the Blues last played host to a Stanley Cup Final game. On May 5, 1970 to be exact, the Blues lost to these same Boston Bruins 6-2 at The Arena. Well, 49 years later, the Blues were Cup Final hosts once more. It wasn't worth the wait.

Three days after recording their first-ever Stanley Cup Final victory, the Blues fell well short of their first-ever home Cup Final win — losing 7-2 to the Bruins before 18,789 at Enterprise Center.

The Bruins sure know how to spoil a party. With the city abuzz with Cup fever, and the crowd as jacked up as it's been all season or maybe in years, the eagerly-anticipated contest turned into a huge letdown.

No amount of celebrities or star athletes in attendance could change the momentum Saturday.

St. Louis actors Jon Hamm and Jenna Fischer were in the house. So was Olympic star Jackie Joyner-Kersee and former St. Louis Rams Isaac Bruce and Chris Long.

Even Kansas City Chiefs quarterback Patrick Mahomes was in the stands, shown on the video board wearing a Blues jersey and chugging a beer.

But Boston had almost as many power-play goals as the Blues had celebrity sightings. The Bruins scored four times with the man advantage — on just four shots — and finished with seven Bruins scoring a goal apiece.

The Blues were missing one of their top penalty-kill players in the suspended Oskar Sundqvist. But 4-for-4?

"There were some deflections," coach Craig Berube said. "Two of them. One went off of (Patrice) Bergeron with a deflection — we didn't get his stick. One went off (Jay) Bouwmeester's stick and in. We've got to be better. Penalty kill's got to be better."

The Blues had been the least-penalized team in the playoffs entering the Cup Final, but you wouldn't know it by what's transpired three games into this series. The Blues have been whistled for 17 penalties in three games, and spent 14 minutes in the box on seven infractions Saturday.

"Well, we do have to limit the penalties for sure," captain Alex Pietrangelo said. "We know they have a dangerous power play and we've been flirting with danger here the whole series, and it burnt us tonight. But in saying that, we've got to do a better job of killing them tonight and we didn't.

"That's why they won the hockey game."

Penalties or not, it wasn't the best night for rookie goaltender sensation Jordan Binnington. He was pulled for the first time in his NHL career after allowing the first five goals.

"I've gotta do a better job of giving us a chance to win," Binnington said. "Three goals in the first, that's never good."

After a quick start for the Blues — Boston didn't even have a shot on goal for the first six minutes — the Bruins scored three times in the first period, including twice in the final 2 minutes 20 seconds.

After Torey Krug made it a 5-1 Boston lead with 7:48 left in the second, Binnington was replaced by Jake Allen. Krug's goal came on the shot that deflected off Bouwmeester's stick.

"My confidence level's really high (in Binnington)," Berube said afterwards. "Five goals he allowed, so he had seen enough. We just wanted to pull him and get him ready for the next game."

Allen had not played at home since a Jan. 8 start against the Dallas Stars. And he hadn't played at all in nearly two months, since a 3-2 shootout loss at Chicago on April 3.

Like the Blues as a whole, Binnington has shown a knack for bouncing back strong after defeats. He'll be put to the test on that front when Game 4 rolls around on Monday.

"It's a loss," Binnington said. "I'm not happy with that. We're going to regroup and prepare for the next game."

"It's not his fault at all," David Perron said. "I'm sure he's disappointed but it has nothing to do (with him). If there's one reason we're here, it's because of him.

"Games like that, we don't want them to happen but it did tonight. Much like the hand pass against San Jose — even though it's a different situation — but we have to find a way to turn the page and come back way better."

The Bruins' Charlie Coyle shoots the puck past Blues goalie Jordan Binnington for Boston's second goal of Game 3. The Blues struggled mightily in a 7-2 loss.

So Boston is up 2-1 in the best-of-seven series, halfway home to its seventh NHL championship. Meanwhile, the Blues must win three of the final four to win their first Cup.

St. Louis trailed San Jose two games to one in the Western Conference Final, and trailed Dallas three games to two in the second round, yet went on to win those series. They'll need another series comeback to take the Cup.

While Binnington struggled, Tuukka Rask was very good in goal Saturday for Boston. Former Blues captain David Backes was a constant agitator in a game that featured all kinds of scrums and skirmishes.

Besides Sundqvist, who'll return for Game 4, the Blues were also missing Robert Thomas (wrist) and Vince Dunn (mouth, head).

There was tremendous energy in the building at the start of the game, and the Blues rode that wave for a while, outshooting the Bruins 5-0 over the first six minutes of play.

But the Bruins gradually took control of the first period — and the game — draining the life out of the building and a fan base that came ready to see history. What they saw instead was one of the Blues' worst postseason losses ever.

The seven Boston goals were the most allowed by the Blues since an 8-3 loss to Detroit in the conference semifinals in 1996. The franchise record for most goals allowed in the postseason is 10 — against these same Bruins in 1972.

Perron bristled when asked if the buildup to this game perhaps resulted in too much nervous energy for the Blues.

"I don't know," he replied. "I don't know. I wasn't nervous."

But could the Blues have been too pumped up for one of the bigger nights in St. Louis sports history?

"You can say a lot of things," he said. "We'll look at some video tomorrow and try to find that out." ∎

BLUES 4, BRUINS 2
JUNE 3, 2019 • ST. LOUIS, MISSOURI

OH, REALLY!

O'REILLY GOALS HELP BLUES TIE THE SERIES, MAKE MORE CUP FINAL HISTORY

BY JIM THOMAS

As usual, the Blues didn't take the most direct route. But here they are, once again tied 2-2 in a best-of-seven series after four games.

They were in the same spot against Winnipeg, Dallas and San Jose, their first three opponents in these playoffs. Luckily for the Blues, Saturday's 7-2 drubbing at the hands of the Boston Bruins counted as only one loss.

"It doesn't matter if you lose 2-1 or 10-1," Oskar Sundqvist said. "A loss is a loss and you need to regroup and refocus. And that's what we did."

If the Blues have shown one thing since late January, when they began their second-half sprint to the playoffs, it's never, ever count them out.

So here they are again after Monday's 4-2 triumph over Boston before 18,805 at Enterprise Center. Once again, it's down to a best-of-three affair, with Game 5 of the Stanley Cup Final on Thursday in Boston.

"Our team responds pretty well to things," coach Craig Berube said. "They have all playoffs. We knew what we had to do tonight — the entire team. First of all, our discipline was a lot better. And second of all — (here he paused) — we were relentless tonight. We didn't stop for 60 minutes. That's how I looked at the game."

The Blues' stars turned in big games, with two goals by Ryan O'Reilly, including the game-winner with 10:38 to play in the third period. Vladimir Tarasenko stayed hot with his 11th goal of this postseason and his sixth in his last eight games.

Captain Alex Pietrangelo played his best game of the postseason. He had two assists, was plus-3 and was stout on defense. He logged 29 minutes 37 seconds of ice time. Yes, he played half the game.

After getting shelled for five goals in little more than 1

1/2 periods Saturday, Jordan Binnington bounced back like he almost always does in his amazing rookie season. He is now 13-2 following games in which he has suffered a loss of any kind all season, and 7-2 under those circumstances in the playoffs.

And Brayden Schenn added an empty-netter to clinch the victory with 1:29 to play.

It all added up to more history, this time the first Stanley Cup Final victory on home ice in franchise history.

"It's been a long time, right?" Pietrangelo said. "The city's been waiting a long time for this. We weren't too proud of last game. ... But you could see the buzz around the city. Driving to the game, it's pretty fun to see. You got the Cardinals guys sitting up there (in the stands), too.

"That's what this city's about. Great sports city. Underrated sports city in my opinion. The fans are great. They never gave up on us all year. Didn't give up in the playoffs. We've been down. They just keep on cheering, keep on supporting us. And we'll put on the best effort we can for them."

But those fans, and the Blues, want a little more.

As the players headed off the ice, chants of "We Want the Cup!" cascaded down from the rafters at Enterprise. Two more Blues victories, and they're there.

"It's anyone's game now," Sundqvist said. "We have to keep doing what we did today."

What they did Monday was avoid the penalty box. After racking up 17 penalties over Games 1-3, they had only three infractions in Game 4. They stayed disciplined, were more decisive with their puck movement, and forechecked like crazy.

After dominating most of the second period, the Blues gave up a shorthanded goal — by Boston defenseman Brandon Carlo — with 5 minutes 41 seconds left in the period. That tied the game at 2-2.

St. Louis Blues center Ryan O'Reilly (90) celebrates his first period goal in the Game 4 win. O'Reilly had two goals in the series-tying victory.

If this were October, November or December, more likely than not the Blues would have folded like a tent after such a score. Those Blues had trouble holding leads, closing out games. They were "fragile" in the words of the coach and some of the players.

But those Blues are a distant memory. These Blues are mentally tough, physically imposing, and borrowing Berube's word — relentless.

"That was a tough one to give up for sure," Berube said of the shorthanded goal. "But I thought our bench was fine. I didn't feel like there was any panic.

"It was unfortunate that that happened. That second period was as good as I've seen us play for a while."

The third period wasn't bad, either. The Blues outshot the Bruins 13-4 in the final period.

For the second time in this series, Boston played most of the game with only five defensemen. This time veteran Zdeno Chara left in the second period after taking a puck to the face and did not return.

The Blues' Vince Dunn returned Monday after missing six games after taking a puck to his face in Game 3 of the San Jose series — the infamous "Hand Pass" game. Dunn had an assist on O'Reilly's first goal of the game, which came on a lightning quick wraparound move just 43 seconds into the contest.

But wouldn't you know it, just a couple of shifts into the game, Dunn took a high stick to the mouth (the other side) that left him with a bloody lip.

"It (stinks)," said Dunn, who said he was still shaking after the game in the excitement of playing his first Cup Final at age 22.

Boston's Charlie Coyle scored his third goal in as many games to tie it 1-1 later in the first, then came Tarasenko's 33rd playoff goal since the start of the 2014 postseason. Only Alex Ovechkin (34) has more in the NHL.

After Carlo's shorty, O'Reilly's fifth goal of the playoffs came on a rebound of a Pietrangelo shot from near the right point.

Boston goalie Tuukka Rask described it as a "Ladies tee shot."

Not sure what that means. But Rask left some rebounds Monday, and O'Reilly made him pay on this one.

"I'm just trying to do what I can to get to that backside," O'Reilly said. "It was just kind of a great bounce, it happens sometimes, and then I just tried throwing it to the net. Sometimes you get those bounces and I was lucky to be on that end of it." ■

Ryan O'Reilly wraps around the goal to score for the Blues just 43 seconds into Game 4.

BLUES 2, BRUINS 1
JUNE 6, 2019 • BOSTON, MASSACHUSETTS

WHAT A TRIP!

BLUES ON THE BRINK OF WINNING FRANCHISE'S FIRST STANLEY CUP

BY JIM THOMAS

Three down, one to go. The Blues are on the doorstep of hockey history, on the brink of winning the franchise's first Stanley Cup.

It came cloaked in some controversy, but Thursday's 2-1 victory over the Boston Bruins at TD Garden gave the Blues a 3-2 lead in the best-of-seven Cup Final. They can clinch with a victory in Game 6 in St. Louis.

Just one more win.

"It's obviously a lot of emotion that goes through your head and stuff like that," Brayden Schenn said. "We've been battling all year, we've been grinding all year. We know what's at stake ... and we're gonna be ready for Game 6."

The Blues got goals from a suddenly-revived Ryan O'Reilly and feisty David Perron. They got one of the best games yet from rookie goalie Jordan Binnington, who stopped 38 of 39 shots. In the process, Binnington continued his own march through playoff history.

His ninth road victory established an NHL record for a rookie goaltender in one postseason. And he tied the NHL rookie record for most overall wins in one postseason at 15, a mark he now shares with four others.

"He was excellent all game, and did a great job in the first period for sure," coach Craig Berube said. "They came hard, Boston. We were tested in the first (period) for sure and 'Binner' stood tall. Big reason we won the game."

The Blues killed off three Boston power plays Thursday, making them 6-for-6 on the penalty kill since allowing four power-play goals in Game 3 Saturday. And they may have benefited most from a penalty that wasn't called.

Midway through the third period, with the Blues up 1-0, Tyler Bozak came at Boston's Noel Acciari from behind. Bozak stuck out his stick and appeared to touch the puck, Acciari fell backward and the crowd at TD Garden, not to mention

everyone on the Boston bench, thought it should have been a tripping penalty.

But there was no call by referees Steve Kozari and Kelly Sutherland. Seconds later, Perron scored his seventh goal of the postseason but first of this series on an attempted pass that deflected off Boston goalie Tuukka Rask and into the net.

"It's not like something crazy was missed in my opinion," Perron said of the no-call. "I don't know."

The crowd thought otherwise, showering the ice with debris.

"It was a little puck battle," Bozak said. "I went for the puck with my stick and it kinda got caught in his feet. I don't know. And then we just got the puck back. DP (Perron) tried to pass it and it banked in off Rask and went in. So we'll take it."

Bruins coach Bruce Cassidy didn't take it — lightly, that is — when it came to the no-call.

"The narrative changed after Game 3," Cassidy said. "There's a complaint or whatever put forth by the opposition. It just seems to have changed everything."

That was a reference to some mild complaining by Berube following his team's 7-2 loss in Game 3 about the amount of penalties being called against the Blues.

In stark contrast to Berube after the "Hand Pass" game against San Jose, when the Blues coach said very little about that blown call in overtime, Cassidy had plenty to say about the Bozak no-call.

"Their player is on his way to the box," Cassidy said. "It's right in front of the official. ... The spotter took (Acciari) out of the game for a possible concussion. I mean, it's blatant. It had a big effect on the game."

Cassidy went on to say that the NHL is "getting a black-eye" with their playoff officiating and said the no-call on Bozak was "egregious."

The NHL eventually apologized for the blown call on

In a controversial play leading up to the winning goal in Game 5, Tyler Bozak tripped the Bruins' Noel Acciari — but there was no call.

the hand pass by San Jose. At the start of the Cup Final, commissioner Gary Bettman said his head almost exploded when he saw that play.

There were no apologies from the NHL on Thursday night.

NHL senior vice president and director of officiating Stephen Walkom said this about Thursday's no-call to a pool reporter after the game:

"We don't make comments on judgment calls within games. There are hundreds of judgment calls in every game. The official on the play, he viewed it and he didn't view it as a penalty at the time."

So the Blues had a 2-0 lead with 9:24 to go, but not for long. With the Blues about to get whistled for a delayed penalty, Jake DeBrusk fired from the right faceoff circle and beat Binnington. With 6:28 to play it was a 2-1 game and TD Garden came alive.

But the Blues weathered the storm down the stretch, continuing their road warrior ways. It was their ninth victory in 12 away games this postseason. In the history of the Stanley Cup, only five teams have won more in a single postseason.

"Probably not as pretty as we'd like it to be, but we gutted it out and got the job done," Schenn said. "Binner played unbelievable for us. They took it to us for most of that game. We sat back maybe a little too much, and we're gonna have to change that for Game 6."

Bozak agreed.

"They pushed hard in the first, the second and the third," he said. "I think Binner really held it down for us. And we got a couple late for him."

Well, actually the game's first goal — O'Reilly's — came just 55 seconds into the second period.

The line of Zach Sanford-O'Reilly-Perron has been together for only 14 games — regular season and playoffs combined — but they ended Game 5 with 14 goals and 27 assists in those games with the first goal coming on a dazzling between-the-legs backhand pass from Sanford to O'Reilly.

Sanford's pass was between two sets of legs — his own and then Boston defenseman Charlie McAvoy — with O'Reilly on the receiving end in front of the net. O'Reilly's backhand beat Rask top shelf.

And helped put the Blues just one win away from hockey history. ◼

Jordan Binnington stops a wraparound attempt by Boston's Brad Marchand during the third period. Binnington stopped 38 of 39 shots in the Blues' 2-1 victory.

BRUINS 5, BLUES 1
JUNE 9, 2019 • ST. LOUIS, MISSOURI

ON THE ROAD AGAIN

BRUINS FORCE GAME 7 IN BOSTON

BY JIM THOMAS

The moment was there for the St. Louis Blues. The bright and shiny Stanley Cup in the house. Anticipation high. The franchise's 52-year wait almost over.

It's not over yet.

The Boston Bruins spoiled the party Sunday night, defeating the Blues 5-1 at Enterprise Center.

The Bruins were opportunistic on offense and air-tight on defense. When challenged by the Blues, goalie Tuukka Rask was up to the challenge.

So this Stanley Cup Final series is now tied 3-3 with a deciding Game 7 Wednesday at TD Garden in Boston.

"Listen, if you told me four months ago we were going to be in the Finals in Game 7, I think I'd take it," coach Craig Berube said. "We've been a good road team. We've won twice up there in this series, so we're a confident group."

Nothing has come easy for the Blues this season, and that's certainly the case this postseason. The Blues were down two games to one in the Western Conference Final against San Jose after the Hand Pass game - and won the next three.

They were down 3-2 against Dallas in Round 2 and facing elimination in Game 6 at American Airlines Center. They won the next two to close out the series.

Even in Round 1 against Winnipeg they were in danger of losing their third game in row, but rallied from a 2-0 deficit in the third period for a Game 5 win and then won the series in six.

Now they must win a Game 7 in Boston to win their first Stanley Cup ever.

"We've got a lot of work ahead of us and we're confident," said Ryan O'Reilly, who scored the Blues' only goal. "We're a great road team. That's our story. We gotta get it done on the road."

But for the seventh time in 13 postseason home games, the Blues couldn't get it done at Enterprise. It certainly wasn't for lack of fan support.

"It was crazy," David Perron said. "We stayed at the hotel (near Enterprise) in the afternoon, and you could hear people honking and yelling, 'Let's Go Blues!' You could see people walking up and down the street. It was a cool sighting. ..."

As the final seconds ticked down on Sunday, the crowd of 18,890 chanted "Let's Go Blues!" and "We Want the Cup!" after the team's final home game of the season.

Don't confuse this game with the Blues' 7-2 shellacking in Game 3 here June 1. The Blues had a good start, gave up a 5-on-3 power-play goal 8 minutes 40 seconds into play, but trailed only 1-0 entering the third period.

"I thought it was an even game, really," Berube said. "Two periods, it's tight hockey. There's not a lot of room out there.

"I'll credit Boston. They played well. They checked well. They didn't give us a ton of room out there. I didn't think we gave them much either. Can we play better? Yeah, we can play better. But I thought we handled the pressure (of the moment) pretty well."

The game — and the Cup — were there for the taking as the period began. But the Blues couldn't take them.

Just 2½ minutes into the third, Bruins defenseman Brandon Carlo sent a knucklepuck toward Jordan Binnington from just inside the blueline. It took a bad hop as it approached Binnington and went in for a 2-0 lead.

It was a huge goal, especially considering how well Rask and the Boston defense were playing.

Binnington was testy when asked what happened on the goal.

"Did you watch it?" Binnington asked a reporter.

(Yes, was the reply.)

"Did it bounce?" Binnington asked.

(Yes, was the reply.)

"Good eye," Binnington said.

Midway through the third, it became 3-0 Boston when 23-year-old Karson Kuhlman beat Binnington far side.

O'Reilly gave the Blues a pulse when his fourth goal in three games trimmed the lead to 3-1. But just two minutes

Bruins teammates celebrate after David Pastrnak (not shown) scored late in Game 6 to put the Blues in a 4-1 hole.

later, with 5:54 left to play, David Pastrnak scored the first even-strength goal of the series for the Bruins' top line — the "Perfection Line" it's called.

And that was it for Game 6, with Zdeno Chara adding an empty-netter with 2:19 left to close out the scoring.

"It obviously wasn't good enough," O'Reilly said of the Blues' performance. "Obviously not the start that we wanted. Bad play by myself there to take the penalty and take it to 5-on-3.

"It took the wind out of our sails and it took too long for us to climb back in. Their second goal was a lucky bounce. Just kind of bounced up on Binner. Not much we could do there. We just didn't respond the right way."

Given the potent Boston power play, the Blues have stressed all series the importance of staying out of the box and avoiding silly penalties. Well, Brayden Schenn was sent to

the box for boarding at the 7:17 mark of the first, and then 62 seconds later O'Reilly joined him — sending the puck over the glass for a delay of game penalty.

After just 21 seconds of 5-on-3 play, the Bruins were on the board on Brad Marchand's back-door one-timer.

Special teams have been a problem for the Blues throughout this series, and Sunday was no different. The Blues went 0-for-4 on the power play, running their tally to 1-for-18 for the series. Meanwhile, the Bruins are 7-for-21 on the power play this series.

Without the special teams domination, this series would be over and the Blues would be Cup champions.

"We had 12 shots (on the power play)," Berube said. "We did have momentum, we had some good looks. We didn't score. Rask made some good saves. Can it be better? Yeah, it has to be better. ... We've definitely got to bury a couple." ▪

BLUES 4, BRUINS 1
JUNE 12, 2019 • BOSTON, MASSACHUSETTS

AT LAST

THE ST. LOUIS BLUES ARE FIRST!

BY JIM THOMAS

Stanley met Gloria on Wednesday night in TD Garden, and for Blues fans everywhere it's a match made in hockey heaven.

The wait is over, the curse lifted. After 52 years, the St. Louis Blues are Stanley Cup champions for the first time by virtue of their 4-1 victory over the Boston Bruins in Game 7.

Rookie goalie Jordan Binnington kept the game from slipping away in the first period, when the Blues went more than 16 minutes without a shot on goal and the Bruins pelted him with 12 shots.

Conn Smythe Trophy winner Ryan O'Reilly gave the Blues a lead they'd never lose with a tip-in goal late in the first period. Captain Alex Pietrangelo, Brayden Schenn and finally Zach Sanford followed with goals to make it a 4-0 game in the third period. The defense held firm in front of Binnington, and it was all over but the shouting.

There was plenty of shouting, cheering, hugging, tears on the ice afterwards. It was mayhem, the happiest type of mayhem imaginable.

There was Pat Maroon, the pride of Oakville, with son Anthony. Colton Parayko, handing the Stanley Cup to young Laila Anderson, who's battling a rare disease.

The "Sasky Boys" — Saskatchewan natives Brayden Schenn and Jaden Schwartz — posing with the Cup in front of several hundred Blues fans who somehow found their way into the Garden.

And Pietrangelo, pausing as he spoke to reporters on the ice to listen to chants of "Let's Go Blues! Let's Go Blues!" He goes down in history as the first Blues player to lift the Cup.

"Heavier than I thought," Pietrangelo joked. "My first thought was make sure Bouw (Jay Bouwmeester) gets an opportunity because that's what you work for. You work for your teammates."

Bouwmeester, a 16-year vet who went his first 10 years in the league without playing in a single playoff game, was the first to get the Cup from Pietrangelo. And then Alexander Steen, Chris Thorburn, David Perron ... and on it went.

The Blues have the Cup.

"It means the world to me," Maroon said. "To bring it back home to St. Louis, it can't be better. And being from St. Louis and being with those fans when I was young. And even when I played in the National Hockey League for other teams, I still watched those Blues and how they suffered — and how those fans suffered.

"Not anymore. We did it!"

Yes they did. It actually happened. You can say it, shout it. The Blues are Stanley Cup champions, going from worst to first in one season.

No team in the four major North American team sports (NHL, NBA, NFL, MLB) had ever been in last place overall even one-quarter into a season and gone on to make the league championship series (or in the case of the NFL, the Super Bowl).

The Blues, last in points on the morning of Jan. 3, have gone one better. They've won the whole thing.

It probably doesn't happen without O'Reilly, who has been playing with a rib injury for much of these playoffs. That's the reason why his faceoff wins dropped dramatically and his shot seemed to lack its usual zip.

"He was the guy that kind of kept us afloat a little bit at the start of the year," Bouwmeester said. "He was probably the one consistent guy that was playing at a high level. ... right from the start he was lights out."

Blues players Jaden Schwartz and Brayden Schenn hug goalie Jordan Binnington after clinching the Stanley Cup. Binnington withstood an offensive onslaught in the first period and kept the Bruins scoreless for most of Game 7.

There's no doubt O'Reilly helped get them across the finish line. His first-period goal gave him eight points in the series (five goals, three assists), a Blues record for a Stanley Cup Final. His 22 points in the playoffs on eight goals and 14 assists set another Blues record.

What a journey it's been for O'Reilly with the Blues. As he sat at the podium with the Conn Smythe Trophy at his side, O'Reilly hearkened back to July 1 when he spoke to Blues general manager Doug Armstrong on the phone after being traded to St. Louis from Buffalo.

"I'm looking at the roster, I was so amped up," O'Reilly said. "I just said, 'Let's go win a Cup.'"

And here they are.

With just 3:13 left in the first period, he tipped in a Bouwmeester shot from near the blueline for the game's first goal. As such he became only the third player in Stanley Cup Final history to score his team's opening goal in four consecutive games, joining Sid Smith in 1951 and Norm Ullman in 1966.

With just 7.9 seconds left in the period, the Blues struck again. Jaden Schwartz carried the puck out of the neutral zone past the blueline, eluding a would-be check to keep the play alive. Near the goal line, Schwartz passed back to Pietrangelo, who skated in patiently on Tuukka Rask and beat the Boston goaltender with a backhand for a 2-0 lead.

It was Pietrangelo's third goal of the postseason; he also had a secondary assist on the O'Reilly goal. So he extended his totals to 16 assists and 19 points — both Blues records for a defenseman in a single postseason.

"Great play by Schwartzy; Schenner backs their 'D' off and lets me drive the lane," Pietrangelo said. "It was a big goal at the time, but those last two really pushed us over the edge."

That would be the third-period goals by Schenn and Sanford to spoil the Garden party.

Binnington did the rest, keeping the Blues in the game in the first period, and keeping the Bruins off the scoreboard until just 2 minutes 10 seconds remained to play. He entered the game 7-2 this postseason following a loss, with a 1.86 goals-against average and a .933 save percentage.

Make that 8-2 after Wednesday.

"We know he's going to be ready," Pietrangelo had told reporters before Game 7. "You guys have seen the way he goes about his business. I'm not too worried about him."

As things turned out there was no reason to worry. Not at all. ◼

Craig Berube kisses the Stanley Cup as his players cheer him on. Berube took over the Blues' head coaching job in November when the team was near the bottom of the NHL standings, and he guided it to the franchise's first championship.

ROAD TO
THE CUP

DEFENSEMAN

ALEX PIETRANGELO

NEW PARENT TO TRIPLETS, PIETRANGELO ALSO GIVES BLUES A GUIDING HAND
BY TOM TIMMERMANN • SEPTEMBER 30, 2018

The Blues made four big offseason acquisitions — Ryan O'Reilly, Tyler Bozak, David Perron and Pat Maroon — though captain Alex Pietrangelo looks at it as only three. "(Perron) doesn't even count," Pietrangelo said. "It's the third time around."

Threes seem to be following Pietrangelo around everywhere nowadays. Those additions for the Blues, moves that can take the team from playoff outsider to Stanley Cup contender, are only the second-most important trio of new faces for Pietrangelo this offseason. In July, he and his wife, Jayne, became parents of triplets, welcoming, in order, Theodore, Oliver and Evelyn into the world. At two months, all are doing well, and that includes the overworked parents.

"It's been a busy offseason for myself, and the team," Pietrangelo said.

If Pietrangelo went through a major change two years ago when he became Blues captain, a job that carries all sorts of responsibilities, that's nothing compared to the responsibilities that come with having triplets.

"It's different, especially when you go from zero to three," he said. "Best thing that's ever happened to me, though. It's hard to argue with that. Anybody that's a parent knows that feeling. Like anything, it's a lot of work, but it's pretty fun going home every day and seeing them.

"You have one, you have two, obviously three's a lot more work. You have to be pretty disciplined in your scheduling. You have your routine, you've got to stick to the routine. It took a couple weeks to figure that out, but we've kind of got that down now."

It's also a big reversal for Alex and Jayne because not long before, they were dealing with the loss of Gabriel Pietrangelo in June 2017 to complications during pregnancy. "The single greatest thing we've ever been given was taken away from us, just like that," Pietrangelo wrote in the Players' Tribune in March.

Now, the family has been given a new start.

"Obviously the end result has been three little miracles, as I call them," he said. "It was tough getting to this point. That's why we love them as much as we do, because it's been such a long road to get where we are. Here we are. We didn't think it would be three at once, but here we are.

"You're going to love them either way, but you love them even more. Sometimes it's hard to explain why things happen, but sometimes the end result is OK."

For a lot of athletes, they don't really grow up until they become parents, until they have a house to go home to with a little kid waiting for them. That is not the case for Pietrangelo, who will turn 29 in January, but the children have brought a seriousness to life, despite the boyish looks and big grin he's had since he was a newcomer to the NHL. This will be his third season as captain of the Blues, and it's a case where it seems it was a job he was born for.

"Yeah, his maturity has gone up three times," joked coach Mike Yeo. "I would say that's a life-changing event, there's no question. Just the way you look at everything, the way that you see things from a day-to-day basis, it changes when you have kids. This is relatively new for him still, but I would say that I've seen a difference in him, and maybe that's part of it."

Defenseman and team captain Alex Pietrangelo takes the ice for pregame introductions before the home opener between the St. Louis Blues and the Dallas Stars.

Part of that is not Theodore, Oliver and Evelyn. It's Ryan, Tyler and Pat.

"I also think there's two other parts," Yeo said. "One, we have a lot of turnover and a lot of change, and I think that's helped Petro in a sense. That he comes in and he just sort of knows his spot. He knows that he has to take over and take control of the group. And I also say just sort of his maturity in the role of being a captain, you can see his development there. You can see he has another level to his confidence and his leadership."

The improvements for Pietrangelo are not just on offense, even if the team's defensive group stayed intact.

"I'd say it's depth on both ends of the ice," he said. "If you look at the way 'O'Rei' takes draws, his responsibility on the penalty kill, the defensive zone, the way he plays all situations; Patty's a big body, takes care of both ends of the ice; Bozie's a right-handed centerman. Not only did we add guys that can bring an offensive upside, which obviously we need, but they care about the other end of the ice, which our foundation is built on, has been like that for years. The depth throughout the entire lineup is the best I've seen in a while."

Pietrangelo's first two seasons as captain have brought challenges. In the first, coach Ken Hitchcock got fired in midseason, and Pietrangelo had to guide the team through rough waters. Then last season, the team struggled in the wake of injuries and letdowns and failed to make the playoffs for the first time in six seasons. When that happens, the captain takes responsibility.

"I'm the one who's supposed to lead the charge, right, and we fell short," he said. "You feel like that responsibility falls on you. Now you have new acquisitions and the responsibility to get everyone on the same page and make sure everyone understands what the ultimate goal is, and it hasn't been an issue. We got some real good character guys, so it's made my life easy. Next job is to translate it on to the ice."

It is something, he has found, that you can't do alone. He calls Jayne "an angel" for the work she has to put in with the kids while he's playing hockey, and he doesn't hesitate to pitch in to help wherever needed. He's embraced everything from changing diapers on up, and you'd better believe that with three newborns, there are a lot of diapers.

"It takes a team, trust me," he said.

He was talking about parenting, but he just as well could have been talking about the Blues. ■

Alex Pietrangelo's leadership was essential in a season which featured a head coaching change and a unified charge from worst in the league to playoff contention.

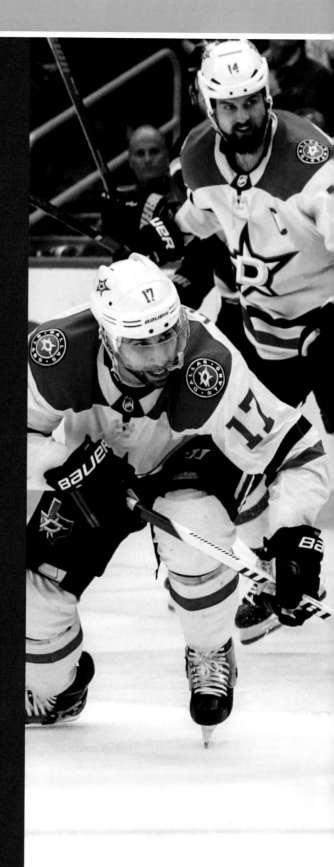

57
LEFT WING

DAVID PERRON

PERRON PROSPERS IN BIGGER ROLE SINCE CLEARING THE AIR WITH BLUES COACH
BY JIM THOMAS • JANUARY 17, 2019

About the last thing David Perron expected when he signed a four-year, $16 million free-agent contract with the Blues in July was that he'd have a new coach before Thanksgiving.

And surely he didn't expect that the new coach, one Craig "Chief" Berube, would make him a healthy scratch after just eight games on the job.

"Obviously, you never want to go through that again," Perron said. "But it's definitely how you respond."

Man, has Perron responded. The 12-year vet from Sherbrooke, Quebec, has nine goals and nine assists in 17 games since being scratched for the Blues' game Dec. 9 against Vancouver. He's currently in the midst of a 12-game point streak, tied for fifth-longest by any NHL player this season.

As Perron spoke in a hallway Wednesday at the Boston University rink, where the Blues held an optional skate, several teammates walked by.

"There he is, the hottest player in the league," said one of those players, Pat Maroon.

To say Perron's improved production is a direct result of the Vancouver scratch, well, that's not exactly true. Perron did have five points (three goals, two assists) in the six games preceding his benching.

But Berube didn't like some of the penalties Perron was taking. For his part, Perron wasn't thrilled with his role on the team.

"The conversations that I had with Chief were very important," Perron said. "A lot of the things I'll keep between him and I, but just kind of explaining what I went through last year. And how I felt when you feel important. Those type of things, you know what I mean? When you feel important you can play (better)."

Exposed by the Blues in the expansion draft and claimed by Vegas, Perron had a bigger-than-usual role with the Golden Knights.

It worked out well for both parties: Vegas made the Stanley Cup Finals and Perron registered a career high 66 points on 16 goals and 50 assists.

So part of Perron's frustration with the Blues was a lesser role with a struggling team.

"I felt like I proved a little bit of something last year with having a bigger role (for Vegas)," Perron said. "A role that I never had pretty much in my career, and did good with that. And we had success as a team, too.

"So I wanted to bring that here, obviously. I didn't get that right away."

But he is now. In 27 games before Vancouver, Perron was averaging 15 minutes, 53 seconds of ice time per game. In 17 games since Vancouver, he's averaging 18:45.

The Blues are 7-4-1 during Perron's point streak, and he's plus-8. With 17 goals this season, already one more than his Vegas total, he has a chance to eclipse his career high of 28 in 2013-14 for Edmonton. His Blues best of 21 goals in 2011-12 certainly is within reach.

"His poise with the puck is unreal," linemate Zach Sanford said. "You see him, he's not the fastest skater but he's really

David Perron tangles with Boston Bruins defenseman Torey Krug during Game 1 of the Stanley Cup Final.

strong on his skates. He's really good with the puck, especially in those areas in tight. Winning those battles and being able to spin off guys and create those chances.

"Obviously he's been doing that a lot for us lately and he's been able to come up big in those clutch moments. Scoring a big goal to tie it up (against the New York Islanders) and get us that point.

"It's just fun to watch and fun to play with when a guy's playing like that with all the confidence in the world. He's dangling, he's protecting the puck, he's doing a lot of things right out there."

It's hard enough for a team to make one big strike in terms of offseason moves. But the Blues made two in signing Perron in free agency and trading for Ryan O'Reilly. They haven't always been on the same line. Remember, the original plan was to have O'Reilly center for Vladimir Tarasenko.

But O'Reilly and Perron have been on the same line for the past 14 games and 21 games total this season. Who knows where the .500 Blues (20-20-5) would be without them this season? The mesh came almost instantly.

"Certain guys, it just happens like that," Perron said. "In my career, there's guys where it worked and guys where it didn't work. He's very similar to (Ryan) Getzlaf in some of the plays he makes. The assist he made (Tuesday) night was unbelievable."

Perron has assisted on O'Reilly's last three scores.

"He's playing phenomenal," O'Reilly said. "He's one of those guys that he gets the puck and he can find everybody. He's got great vision but protects the puck so well. ... He's been on fire and he's been working for it. You see how hard he works out there. He's a big reason why we've won these last few games."

Perron plays with passion, a passion that frequently jumps out at you from the ice.

Part of that passion comes from knowing that nothing is guaranteed. Perron cited an ill-fated stretch for parts of two seasons in Pittsburgh where things didn't go well.

"You almost feel like you're gonna be out of the league in a year or two if you don't figure it out real quick," he said. "I had to dig real deep within myself and kinda look at myself in the mirror with where can I get better — things like that."

If he could do that, then what's a one-game benching?

"I only heard good things about Chief and it's been unbelievable so far," Perron said. "Even though he scratched me, we all love him in here. It has nothing to do with others, there's no hard feelings. We want to go through a wall for him." ∎

David Perron clears the puck away from the boards during the Blues' second-round playoff series against the Stars. Teammates have praised Perron's puck handling and skating ability.

90
CENTER

RYAN O'REILLY

BLUES' ALL-STAR ALWAYS PUSHING TO BE A BETTER PLAYER
BY TOM TIMMERMANN • JANUARY 26, 2019

In the locker room at the Staples Center in Los Angeles, Blues center Ryan O'Reilly sat in a stall, leaning back as far as he could and looking very defeated because, at that moment, that's what he was.

The Blues had lost to the Kings — the Kings! — 4-3 in the kind of defeat that is a total downer. It's two points the Blues desperately needed and two points it looked like the Blues would get when they went up 2-0 late in the first period, and two points they didn't.

As a small group of reporters come over to talk to O'Reilly, the Blues center is about to come face-to-face with his harshest critic: himself.

To O'Reilly, every game, every win or loss, is a referendum on his play. In discussing the game and what went wrong, it does not take long for O'Reilly to come around to himself, and not in a positive way. He has a distinctive way of talking in these situations. He doesn't just say "I." He says, "I myself," a structure that puts an added emphasis on the speaker. "I myself wasn't good enough defensively," he said. And later: "I know I myself at times, I lost my coverage."

That O'Reilly puts this onus on himself is odd because, in this season, the one member of the Blues who should get the least blame for any of the Blues' ills is O'Reilly. He's off to the All-Star Game this weekend and, until David Perron's recent point blitz, it's hard to imagine who else on the team would have possibly been selected.

O'Reilly has 50 points (18 goals, 32 assists), which is 15 more than Perron, who has the next-highest total on the team. His plus-14 is best on the team (Carl Gunnarsson is next at plus-9). His assist on Wednesday in a 5-1 win over Anaheim gave him a six-game point streak. He's already had one six-game streak this season and another 10-game streak. He's third in the league in faceoff percentage, a number made more important by the number of defensive zone starts he gets.

Those feelings are what drives O'Reilly to be one of the first players on the ice every day and one of the last to come off. It's why he's constantly working on something. He needs to be better. The team is counting on him. He's always been that way.

"I think after games, the competitiveness kind of takes over and I get pretty mad at myself for little plays," O'Reilly said two days later, now sitting more relaxed in his stall at the Honda Center in Anaheim. "There's times in the game where things don't go well, you had a chance to score and you don't, that could have changed the outcome of the game and that's just what comes to mind first, and after games I get a little emotional. I look at it that way.

"I think one of the things I learned at a young age, what my dad always preaches, was you have to self-reflect first. That's the most important thing. If you get a team with guys who self-reflect on what they can do differently, it's going to be a good recipe for improving."

But even though he realizes that his emotions may be a bit extreme at times, he thinks that's an attitude he needs to embrace. It provides him with a blueprint for better play.

"I don't think I should change that," he said. "It pushes me to grow my game and make adjustments, and I think in every game I play I think I can make an impact to help change the outcome.

Ryan O'Reilly passes the puck away after stealing it from San Jose Sharks defenseman Joakim Ryan during the Western Conference Final.

"When I say I need to be better in a game, I try to work on that area the next time I'm on the ice. I think last game I was disappointed with the way I defended. I wasn't good away from the puck. … I want to respond with a good defensive performance. Obviously offensively too, to make an impact, but I need to play a lot better away from the puck, especially for a guy that plays a lot of minutes. If I'm doing that, that's going to make it hard on the other team a lot. It's one of those things I think I need to do."

All that makes things complex for O'Reilly in his second career All-Star trip. The Blues season so far has been, by any standard, disappointing. But for the player who is on the ice more than any other forward — by two minutes per game — he sees it all coming back to him. How good can he be playing if the team is struggling so much?

"Absolutely," he said. "I think it's different if you're a guy getting called up. I'm involved in every situation. If the penalty kill's not doing good, I'm a big part of that. If the power play's not doing good, I'm a big part of that. Five-on-five. I can't make anyone else do anything. I can take care of my game. If I do that, that's going to help other guys play better. We all have to do that. We all have to bring our best game and put that forward and when we do it, we can see how dangerous it is and the consistency we're fighting for. And as of late it has been better. The game against LA there were opportunities to win. It's not like we were terrible, it's just our defensive part of the game killed us and I was a big part of that.

"Growing up, I've always been a guy that got to play a majority of the game and I can't get mad at anyone else for not doing their job when I've had plenty of opportunities. Sometimes I need to get a couple of goals, sometimes I don't need to. Sometimes I have to play well defensively and it's good enough to win the game. There's always something you can do different or change or be better at to impact the game and some nights it calls for it more than others. A game where we're beat up and don't have energy, I look at it as a challenge for myself to have an exceptional game. That started at a young age and I don't think I'll change that. That's something that drives me."

It's a drive that shows no signs of letting up, and one he embraces. And the constant working on his game, the constant practice, comes with one other benefit.

When O'Reilly spends extra time on the ice at the end of practices, he's often joined by younger members of the team. The youngsters like the chance to learn from a veteran; playing with the kids makes O'Reilly feel younger.

"I think you always have to be a student of the game and reinvent yourself and keep that beginner's mindset as much as you can," he said. "So being around the young guys and feeding off their energy and what they bring helps keep me young. I used to be the young guy and now I'm looking at them and trying to keep up."

It's a race that Ryan O'Reilly doesn't want to lose. ∎

Ryan O'Reilly played a major role in the Blues' comeback from last place in January while setting an example for younger players on the team.

TUESDAY NIGHT FEVER

DISCO MAKES A COMEBACK AFTER BLUES COMPLETE THEIRS

BY JIM THOMAS • FEBRUARY 6, 2019

In case you haven't noticed, but you probably have, the Blues haven't exactly been the Comeback Kids this season. Through their first 50 games, they had trailed 22 times entering the third period.

Their record in those games? A regrettable 1-18-3. The lone win was back on Dec. 11 in St. Louis, when after trailing the Florida Panthers 1-0 entering the third, the Blues rallied for a 4-3 win.

On Tuesday before an intimate gathering at BB&T Center, it happened again. Trailing 1-0 after two periods to Florida, and then 2-0 just 30 seconds into the third, the Blues got goals from Colton Parayko on a wraparound, Ryan O'Reilly in a mad scrum, and then the game-winner from Vince Dunn to pull out a dramatic 3-2 victory.

And they celebrated with ... disco music. Yes, the sounds of "Gloria" by Laura Branigan were blaring in the visitors' locker room.

"'Gloria's' I guess our song now," Dunn said.

Come again?

"It's a heck of a song," O'Reilly said. "We like it. We got some old souls here."

And he wasn't talking about the nearly 20 fathers and grandfathers who are accompanying the team on the annual Dad's Trip. This is the fourth time the Blues have done this and the team is now 6-1 in this setting. No one wants to disappoint his father, right?

According to Associated Press, "Gloria" became a Blues postgame favorite in part because of a bar in South Philadelphia: Jacks NYB, a private club in the middle of Flyers country. Five Blues players were there Jan. 6 to watch a NFL playoff game between the Eagles and Chicago Bears. A club patron kept yelling "Play 'Gloria'" and a DJ obliged by playing it during every commercial break.

The customers "just went nuts when they heard it, and we loved watching it," Blues forward Robby Fabbri told an AP reporter. "So we just happened to get a win the next day (against the Flyers) and made it our win song." ∎

Blues fans watching from Market Street celebrate Ryan O'Reilly's go-ahead goal during Game 4 of the Stanley Cup Final.

50 GOALIE

JORDAN BINNINGTON

LONG AND WINDING ROAD: BINNINGTON'S PATH TO STARTING GOALIE HAD ITS DETOURS

BY JIM THOMAS • APRIL 10, 2019

For a few years, the Red Dog had Jordan Binnington by a minute.

"The funniest part was, I played one game. I played 13 minutes," Greg Redquest, aka the Red Dog, said. "And before this, Binner had only played 12 minutes. So I still had the title."

Redquest, once Binnington's goalie coach in junior hockey at Owen Sound and still a good friend, played his one and only NHL game in goal for the Pittsburgh Penguins during the 1977-78 season. Again, for 13 minutes.

Until this season, Binnington had played only one NHL game — for the St. Louis Blues — during the 2015-16 season. For 12 minutes and change.

So it was a good joke among friends for a while. But as the seasons went by and Binnington stayed in the minors, maybe it became less funny. Particularly in the fall of 2017 when near the end of Blues camp the team didn't have a place for him in the AHL.

They didn't have an American Hockey League affiliate last season. Instead, they had a loose working arrangement to send players to San Antonio, then a Colorado Avalanche affiliate. The Avalanche could take only one Blues goalie and that goalie turned out to be Ville Husso, who had supplanted Binnington as the top goalie prospect in the organization.

The Blues also had a similar arrangement with the Chicago Wolves, then (and still) a Vegas Golden Knights affiliate. The Wolves didn't need a goalie.

So as a last resort, the Blues wanted to send Binnington to the ECHL — the minor-league hockey equivalent of AA baseball.

At age 24, about the time pro hockey players start to transition from prospect to suspect if they're not in the NHL, Binnington balked at the assignment. Didn't want to go.

"I talked with him for an hour and a half that day when he was going to the 'Coast,'" Redquest said. "He stood by his guns, bless his heart."

A few years earlier with Redquest in the Ontario Hockey League, Binnington had tons of team and individual success. He was a first-team all-star and goaltender of the year in the OHL in the 2012-13 season. In the 2010-11 season, he went 27-12-5 for Owen Sound, leading the Attack to the OHL title, which is a big deal in junior hockey.

He later played for Team Canada in the world junior championships.

"He won every award you can win for a goalie in junior," Redquest said. "The technical ability he had was unbelievable. He just would make saves that were — he'd make them look easy. Good goalies make hard saves look easy. And that's Binner."

Binnington was rated the No. 1 draft-eligible goalie in the OHL when the Blues selected him 88th overall in the 2011 draft. But by September 2017, with the ECHL beckoning, Binnington had reached a career crossroads.

Entering camp in 2017, he was the No. 4 goalie in the Blues' system, behind Husso, Carter Hutton and Jake Allen. The season before, Binnington had fallen behind Husso with the Wolves,

Jordan Binnington blocks a shot from Sharks center Logan Couture during Game 6 of the Western Conference Final.

Jordan Binnington makes a stick save on a shot by Melker Karlsson of the San Jose Sharks.

then the Blues' AHL affiliate, and then coached by Craig Berube.

"I saw the position I was in," Binnington said. "My back was kinda against the wall with the organization. Growing up I was a pretty talented guy. I kind of lost my way from there a little bit.

"So I just sat back and said: 'This is the position you're in. How are you gonna handle it?'

"I was still working hard. But I think my lifestyle habits and choices were just not (conducive) to be a consistent goaltender. I kind of figured out what was important in my life. It's kind of part of growing up, right?

"It took me a little longer than I always wanted, but I'm here. I had a lot of fun, but I didn't like where I was in my career. I think it all comes from just lifestyle, and trying to find peace of mind, and living well, and taking care of my body. Cut down on the late nights."

He rededicated himself to the game, a process that included hooking up with goalie coach Andy Chiodo at the well-known BioSteel hockey camp the past two summers in Toronto.

Three summers ago, Binnington had gotten to know Chiodo while both were goalies training at BioSteel. They hit it off. Established a relationship. But then Chiodo, 10 years Binnington's elder, retired as a player and become a goalie coach. He's currently a goalie development coach for the Pittsburgh Penguins.

But in the summers, he's a goalie coach at BioSteel — and lo and behold, he's had Binnington as a "pupil" the past two summers.

Chiodo said Binnington "has certainly committed himself in a very deliberate way the last two years in every aspect of his game and life. He's committed himself to raising his standard, to raising the bar in every aspect.

"We've been able to spend that time together in the summer where you don't have games … and travel. You can really address different areas of your game and your approach that you want to grow in."

For the past two offseasons, they've done so — from May to August.

"He moves incredibly well, he's got great instincts, he's competitive," Chiodo said. "Really, the level that he's playing at has always been inside him in some way, and we have just worked together to bring it to life."

Of course, that includes working on technical aspects of goaltending.

"But I think it's about developing the whole person," Chiodo said. "It goes well beyond Xs and Os.

"It's about getting the best out of yourself — and that's mentally, emotionally, technically. From a lifestyle standpoint. Your process. There's so many moving parts that contribute to being a successful NHL-er, and sometimes it's just about putting all of that together.

"Putting that whole professional package together to clear the way for his best self to show up. And I think that's kind of what's happened. And it's gonna be an ongoing thing. There's challenges that will present themselves every day. New challenges every week."

Though his path to the NHL took longer than he hoped, Jordan Binnington made the most of his rookie season, capturing the starting job and then a Stanley Cup.

The challenge this week, of course, is Mark Scheifele, Patrik Laine, Kyle Connor, Blake Wheeler and the rest of the Winnipeg Jets in the first round of the Stanley Cup playoffs.

The challenge in the fall of 2017 was that pending ECHL assignment and the task of arresting his slide on the Blues' organizational depth chart.

"When you go into a year, you want to have four or five goaltenders in your group, just for injuries," Blues general manager Doug Armstrong said. "It was a perfect storm in a negative way for Jordan quite honestly. We didn't have our own American League affiliate. So we had Husso as our primary (prospect) goaltender at that time.

"We wanted to put (Husso) in with the core of our players that we were sending to San Antonio. And we had to, for (lack of) a better term, farm Jordan out to a place where we thought he'd get some games. And that was in Boston's organization — in Providence."

Yes, the Bruins organization agreed to take on Binnington, and that proved to be the way out. Binnington was back in the AHL. He didn't play a ton — after all, the Bruins were more interested in developing their prospects, not somebody else's — in Providence.

But Binnington chipped away. He got a start a week. Sometimes two. Before you knew it, he was an AHL all-star putting up strong, strong numbers for Providence. Another summer of work followed with Chiodi at BioSteel.

And here he is. This season, Husso struggled early for San Antonio and then got hurt. Binnington stepped in, became the No. 1 goalie, played lights out. And then got promoted to St. Louis.

"Though he's a rookie at 25, a lot of goaltenders don't get their first opportunity till 24 or 25," Armstrong said. "So he's really not that far behind in the process. ... He just got there a different way. Sort of like the way we got to 99 points this year."

Binnington has had a strong support staff in St. Louis and San Antonio. He speaks highly of the "Two Daves" — Blues goaltender coach David Alexander and Blues goalie development coach Dave Rogalski.

"Rogalski's been pretty key for me because he really still believed in me the last couple years, when not many people around here did," Binnington said. "He really just stayed with me.

"Dave Alexander's been awesome with me. He's a very intelligent guy. He's just full of knowledge, so I'm trying to listen to him as best I can, and he's doing a great job guiding me in the right direction. Both the Daves have been a big part of my success."

And he thinks the world of Allen, who has been nothing but supportive.

"He's Jake Allen's No. 1 fan," Redquest said. "He says, 'Oh my God, he's such a good guy. He helps me out so much.'"

As for the Red Dog, he's lost the title. Binnington now has him by nearly 1,900 minutes. Not to mention five shutouts, two NHL rookie of the month awards and several franchise records.

That's 1,900 minutes. And counting. ∎

GENERAL MANAGER

DOUG ARMSTRONG

ARMSTRONG'S MOVES WITH BLUES PAYING OFF WHEN IT MATTERS MOST
BY BEN FREDERICKSON • APRIL 13, 2019

Doug Armstrong has a self-imposed rule that borders on superstition.

The Blues' general manager does not conduct media interviews during a postseason series.

He will talk before them.

He will talk after them.

But while series are in the process of being decided, Armstrong prefers to watch. And pace. And pass those painstaking seconds during breaks in the action by taking a quick stroll by the candy station set up in the Bell MTS Place press box to see if there's a chocolate or gummy that offers some sweet distraction while the wait for a more lasting satisfaction looms.

While the Blues toiled with the Jets in a Friday night thriller that tilted for good on another dominant third period that sent the Blues home from Winnipeg up 2-0 in this best-of-seven Western Conference quarterfinal, Armstrong offered a quick nod as he cruised by.

No need for comment.

His decisions are saying everything for him.

Ryan O'Reilly, his eye blackened by a scrum, shared between wins in Winnipeg that this is the best team he's had. The Blues' best all-around player would not have been there to say it without Armstrong trading for him this offseason. During a roller-coaster season that is now steadily climbing, O'Reilly has been the constant. Adding him looks smarter by the game, the latest example arriving Friday, when his third-period goal further dented the confidence of the former Vezina Trophy runner-up Connor Hellebuyck.

When Alex Pietrangelo reflected this week on his team's rise, he mentioned the turn to interim coach Craig Berube as the switch that flipped the script. That plot twist was written by Armstrong. He saw the Blues were at risk of digging a hole too deep to escape. He decided he could not wait to see if this talented group he had assembled would mesh with former coach Mike Yeo. Hard decision. Right decision. Berube's Blues have won more regular and postseason games (32) than any other team since Jan. 1.

As he changed coaches, Armstrong resisted any urges to strip leadership roles from team captain Pietrangelo and alternates Vladimir Tarasenko and Alexander Steen. A statement move like that would have scored points with restless fans. It also would have undermined Berube's decision-making powers as the interim. Instead Armstrong delivered a clear message without a needless poke in the chest. The team's core had one more chance to click. If not, a shakeup would come.

"There's some character in that locker room," Pietrangelo said this week. "We looked hard in the mirror there, especially after the coaching change, knowing that the only place was up from where we were. We felt like we did lose a lot of games early on in the season that were close games, games that maybe we had a chance to win. Games that, if we did, could have put us in a better position."

Their present position is suddenly a prime one.

More than 85 percent of teams that take a 2-0 lead in a best-of-seven series go on to win it. The Blues just became the 93rd team to grab this advantage on the road. Of the 92 that accomplished it before them, 72 went on to win the series.

GM Doug Armstrong oversaw several offseason additions to this Blues team, such as Ryan O'Reilly and David Perron, and made the key decision to change head coaches part-way through the season.

We mentioned O'Reilly, but he was just one of four big-splash additions Armstrong made over an offseason that was supposed to lead here all along, and eventually did, despite some unexpected twists.

David Perron, who returned to the Blues as a free agent, scored the Blues' first goal of the postseason. Tyler Bozak, another free-agent addition, netted the Game 1 winner. After setting up Bozak beautifully for a game-one goal, former free agent Patrick Maroon scored in Game 2. Maroon's assist of Bozak in Game 1 and his powerful punch-in to tie Game 2 might have been the biggest Blues plays of the postseason so far. Remember when there was chatter that Armstrong should release the slow-starting local to send a message? Armstrong stuck with Maroon, just like he stuck with veteran defenseman Jay Bouwmeester, who has been a plus-7 player since January.

And don't forget that Oskar Sundqvist is the Blues' current leader in postseason goals (two) and points (three). He arrived in a 2017 Armstrong trade that flipped fan favorite Ryan Reaves to Pittsburgh in a deal that received mixed reviews, at best, at the time.

At this season's trade deadline, Armstrong did nothing of significance. Some hollered. But the Blues were rolling then, and they are fully healthy now. Not messing with a winning chemistry sure seems to have been the right call.

Even Armstrong's mistake of betting on goalie Jake Allen again entering the season has been sidestepped, thanks to the masked phoenix that is Jordan Binnington. How many other teams have a season-saver hiding on the fourth rung of the preseason depth chart?

As impossible as it once seemed, everything is coming up Armstrong when it matters most.

That's gotta taste pretty sweet. ∎

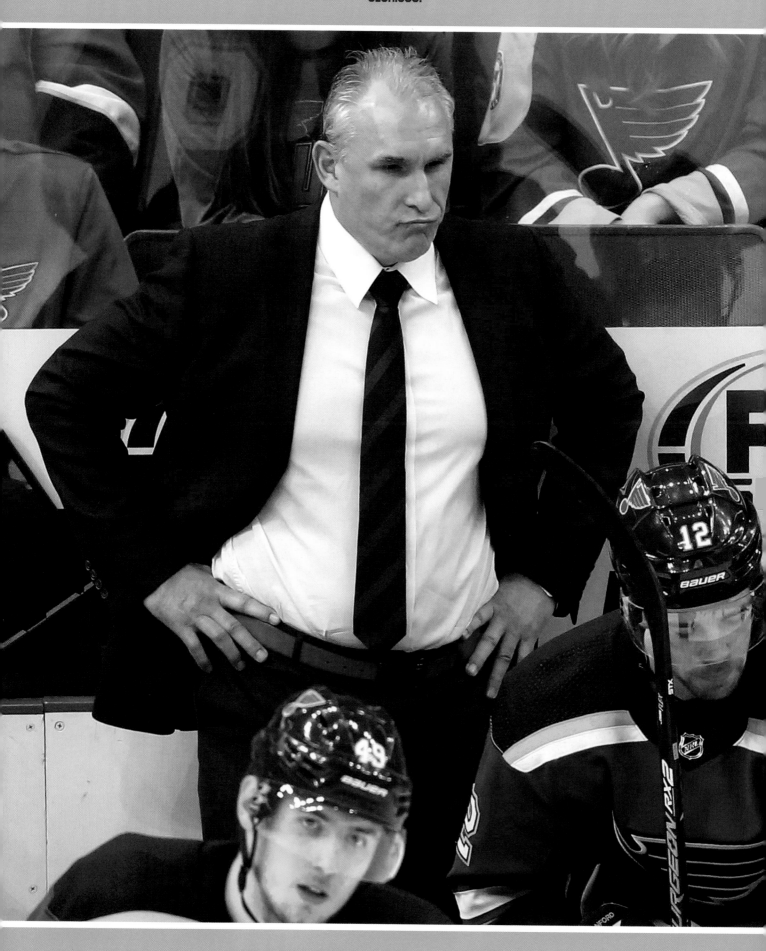

COACH

CRAIG BERUBE

PROUD OF HIS FIRST NATIONS ROOTS, BLUES' BERUBE COULD MAKE STANLEY CUP HISTORY

BY BENJAMIN HOCHMAN • MAY 24, 2019

Calahoo, Alberta, is so small, it's a one-rink hamlet. "It's very tiny — to drive through, it's going to take you 10 seconds," said Blues coach Craig Berube, who improbably ascended from Calahoo to play 17 seasons in the National Hockey League — and now is coaching in the Stanley Cup Final. "You got a general store on the right. Then you got a church, then you got some ball fields, then you got a hockey rink. Then you're out of the town."

Berube grew up on a farm — "Not only grain crops, but cattle," he said — and grew as a hockey player on frozen ponds. In later years, he'd play at the local rink, which is called Calahoo Arena.

"But it might have to get changed to the Craig Berube Rink if he wins the Cup," said Matt Berube, the rink manager, whose father is first cousins with the Blues' coach.

Outside of the rink is a large white sign with red lettering: "Welcome to CALAHOO." Above the words is a logo similar to the old logo of the Cleveland Indians — a man wearing a headdress.

There isn't a local bar or coffee shop in Calahoo — "There's one little table in our general store where you can have coffee," Matt said — but when folks see each other lately, notably at the rink, they're talking about the St. Louis Blues.

"Everybody is so proud to know that he came from here," said Matt, who estimated that "between 75-100" Berubes live in Calahoo or within a 15-kilometer radius.

Craig's own parents — Ramona and Roger Berube — still live in Calahoo. So does Craig's sister. Even in his late 70s, Roger Berube played in a weekly hockey league at Calahoo Arena. Matt described it as an "old-timers league — all the elders in the town and community get together and play." But last fall, at 80, Roger Berube finally had to hang up his skates.

The rink is often busy. The 2016 Canadian Census tallied 85 people in Calahoo itself, but those from Rivière Qui Barre and other nearby hamlets routinely come to play. Many on the ice, just like the coach of the Blues, have native ancestry.

The Canadian counterparts to Native Americans are called First Nations. Craig Berube is Cree. Well, part-Cree. He left Calahoo at 16 and soon picked up the nickname "Chief." A lot of First Nations hockey players picked up the nickname "Chief." Berube said his grandmother "was native," and he grew up playing hockey and baseball with many Cree children.

"What you had to have back then was a Métis card," Berube said of a certified ID card. "It's a half-white, half-native type card. Because, you know, I look white, and I'd go play in these hockey tournaments. They'd want to know if I had native in me. They'd check you out and stuff. Métis is what you call a person that is white and native."

On November 21, 2013, then as the coach of Philadelphia, coach Berube and his Flyers played the Sabres,

Craig Berube watches the action during the Blues' March 12 game against the Coyotes.

coached by Ted Nolan, who is Ojibwe. And so, it was a historic night — the first NHL game in which both coaches were of First Nations descent.

It's believed that if Berube coaches the Blues to a Stanley Cup championship, that will be another first for First Nations.

Sure enough, Nolan's son, Jordan, played 14 games for the Blues this season. While Jordan doesn't dress for the playoff games, he's with the team.

"I am definitely proud of who I am and where I come from," Jordan said. "My dad always instilled that in us growing up. … Ojibwe is Northern Ontario, and there are lots of Cree all over the place. Everyone has their own tribe, depending on where you're from, and some of the remote communities, they still speak their language. But there are not many who speak the language anymore — Ojibwe is rarely spoken on our reserve. And the kids were sent to residential schools and told not to speak their language anymore, so that's how we lost a lot of our language. It's important to keep it."

As for the First Nations communities, Berube succinctly said: "The reserves, some do well, and some don't. Basically the same (as in the United States)."

During summers, Jordan and Ted Nolan have a hockey school. They go to small First Nations communities. They teach some hockey. But really, they're there to share their stories and experiences.

"I think our youth need good role models," Jordan said. "A lot of kids are struggling in these communities, and a lot of them kind of get lost, because lots of them live in the middle of nowhere, and they don't have a way to get out. They really don't have too much guidance. So we try go in there and tell our story.

"Everybody has been through hard times, I've been through hard times. I've been sober now for five years. So it's good for our kids to hear that story. I really just think they need someone they can look up to and say — 'Wow, he was in a place that I was in, so if he can do it, I can do it.' … We're trying to raise good people and good leaders in our community."

Hard to find a better example of a leader than the coach of a team playing for the Stanley Cup.

Craig Berube, a Cree from tiny Calahoo. ∎

Beloved by his players, Craig Berube took over a fractured team in November 2018 and guided the Blues to a Stanley Cup championship.

SUPERHERO

THE LATEST CHAPTER IN LAILA'S STORY, THE DISEASE-FIGHTING, BLUES-INSPIRING SUPERFAN

BY BENJAMIN HOCHMAN • MAY 19, 2019

You feel uncomfortable watching her watching her. The quiet mother taking it all in, while her little girl makes the surreal real, yet again.

The Blues just won Game 4 on Friday night, and there's 11-year-old Laila Anderson, standing on the Blues' bench at Enterprise Center, going live on Channel 5.

Watching Laila's mother, Heather, you can see her brown eyes are tired. It's been a long night. Week. Year. But she's looking at her daughter with this gaze that must feel warm.

"I'm thinking — the boys just won Game 4 of the conference finals, they just tied the series and they are talking to Laila?" Heather said. "She has gone from a fan of the Blues to a friend of the Blues. She has gone from hospital and home isolation to the Blues' bench. She has battled through a long 20 months, just like these boys have battled from the bottom to the top.

"She is my hero."

Laila walks over. Her eyes are wide, as if she refuses to close them.

Laila Anderson, the fighter of the rare disease HLH, a systemic inflammatory syndrome that can be fatal. Her face is now famous. Her story now contagious.

"It's unreal — first it was the support of my family, and then the St. Louis Blues," said Laila, the Blues' logo painted on each of her smiling cheeks. "And now it's all of St. Louis."

The part of the story we know started with the video before Game 3. You've probably seen it. Heather, pointing out to Laila that it's been four months since Laila's been allowed to leave the house. Heather, telling Laila the doctor is "letting up a little." Heather, asking Laila to guess where she gets to go first. Laila, bursting into tears of joy.

But the story began on Halloween. Laila attended a trick-or-treat event with the Blues and Children's Hospital. She met Colton Parayko, one of her favorite players on her favorite team.

"He was 100-percent committed to her, took her around trick-or-treating," Heather said. "I said, 'It's OK,' and he said, 'I've got her — I'm going to hold her bag, I'm going to hold her drink, I'm going to do everything.' He's all in with her — they just have this bond. Ever since then, he's come to visit her in the hospital. Stayed a ridiculously long time. They actually communicate once or twice a week. He just checks on her. It's a genuine friendship.

"They even friended each other on Instagram and send D.M.s. He doesn't friend too many people. It's something special."

Through the organization Be The Match, a donor was found — Laila had a bone marrow transplant in January. She's battled through ensuing chemotherapy. She's fought and fought … and then had more fights to fight.

But the Blues, with the fewest points in the National Hockey League in early January, "have been my inspiration this whole time," Laila said. "And I kind of feel like I'm their inspiration a little. I hope that's the case."

Laila was at Enterprise Center for Game 3. They showed a video of her, pumping up the crowd, filmed at the hospital. If there was a Venn Diagram of Blues fans with goosebumps and Blues fans with tears in their eyes, it would've just been two circles on top of each other.

Laila Anderson, an 11-year-old Blues fan, stands on the bench with her mother, Heather, after the team's Game 4 win against San Jose. Laila is battling HLH, a rare disease, and as the Blues players have supported her, she has ardently cheered on her favorite team.

But the Blues lost Game 3 to San Jose on the infamous hand-pass assist.

"The boys were mad and they wanted to go home — and I didn't want to be down here, I felt bad for them," Heather said. "But we came downstairs anyway. And Colton came out and sat with us — hadn't even showered yet — and talked to us for 30 minutes. Just to see her. He said, 'I'm so proud of you.' She said, 'I just love you.' And he said, 'I love you too, Laila.' Just really good friends.' … She told the players that night, 'It's in the past, boys. Alex (Steen), let's just worry about Friday. Colton, we've got Friday. Let's just focus on Friday.'"

They won on Friday. The Blues tied the series, 2-2. Game 5 is Sunday at San Jose. Game 6 is Tuesday back in St. Louis.

Are Laila and Heather going to Game 6?

"We are — I haven't told her yet," Heather said on Friday night, with Laila standing right next to her.

"We are?" Laila said. "Thank you!"

It was like the video happening again in real life.

"These boys are going to do this," Heather said of the St. Louis Blues, two wins from their first Stanley Cup finals since 1970. "They are going to do it for themselves, for this town and for my kid." ∎

In 2017, Laila Anderson high-fives goalkeeper Carter Hutton after pregame warmups before the Blues' home opener.

17
LEFT WING

JADEN SCHWARTZ

FROM MEXICO TO WINNIPEG AND BEYOND
BY JIM THOMAS • MAY 23, 2019

One of the delights of the Blues' Stanley Cup finals journey has been the unexpected twists and turns along the way.

The unexpected emergence of Oskar Sundqvist, for example. Or the totally unexpected emergence of Jordan Binnington.

Craig Berube's rise from interim head coach — with emphasis on the "interim" — to Jack Adams Award finalist as NHL coach of the year.

How about the fall and rise of Jay Bouwmeester as a bedrock of one of the NHL's top defenses?

The "Big Rig" — Pat Maroon — coming up big in the playoffs for his hometown team, including the ultra-dramatic game-winning goal in double overtime to clinch Round 2 against the Dallas Stars.

OK, one more. How about Jaden Schwartz, the man who went from regular season dud to playoff stud.

Ryan O'Reilly undoubtedly is the team's unofficial MVP for the regular season. Through three rounds of the playoffs, the Blues' postseason MVP has to be Schwartz.

Entering the Stanley Cup finals, most observers consider Boston Bruins goalie Tuukka Rask the favorite for the Conn Smythe Trophy as the NHL's playoff MVP. But Schwartz is right there in the discussion, particularly now that it's golfing season for Logan Couture and the San Jose Sharks.

By now, most ardent Blues fans are familiar with his numbers. Schwartz has more playoff goals (12) in 19 games than he had in 69 regular-season contests (11). He has two postseason hat tricks, and has scored four goals in each of the Blues' postseason series — against Winnipeg, Dallas, and San Jose.

His Game 5-winning goal in the midst of the Winnipeg Whiteout with 15 seconds left in regulation rates as one of the most dramatic goals in Blues postseason history. He batted that one from a couple of feet off the ice into the net.

Winnipeg goalie Connor Hellebuyck referred to it as one of the Blues' "lucky pinballs" that night.

In any event, Schwartz is just one goal behind the "Golden Brett" — Brett Hull — for most goals in a single Blues postseason. Starting with Game 1 Monday of the Stanley Cup finals against Boston, Schwartz has at least four more games to tie or break Hull's postseason record of 13 goals, set in 1990.

How to explain Schwartz's amazing turnaround? Perhaps defensemen Joel Edmundson and Robert Bortuzzo deserve "assists" here.

"We went down to Mexico for our little break, and it just kind of cleared his mind," Edmundson said. "He came back here and he was lights out since."

Schwartz had only three goals for the season when the Blues took their end-of-January break for the All-Star Game and bye period. Players scattered, and Edmundson, Bortuzzo and Schwartz headed to Mexico.

Schwartz had eight goals in 33 regular-season games after the break — not an explosion, but still a 20-goal pace. Then came 12 goals in 19 playoff games. An explosion.

"He's definitely had it in him," Edmundson said. "He was just beating himself up a bit too much. So once he got a couple goals, he's just kept on rolling. And to do this in the playoffs is

Jaden Schwartz picked up his scoring pace in the second half of the regular season, but he reached bold new heights during the Blues' playoff run.

pretty exciting. It's good to see a guy like that be successful."

Schwartz is one of the most intense Blues. Because of that, he brings new meaning to the expression associated with pressing hockey players "squeezing the stick too tight."

"We have a fun dressing room, so guys are trying to loosen him up a bit, and you can definitely tell he's loosened up now," Edmundson said. "He's just having fun playing hockey. That's the best part of this. We're all just having fun playing hockey."

So what happened in Mexico at the end of January to clear Schwartz's mind?

"Just the sun and beaches," Edmundson said. "A couple cocktails. That's about it."

Just as a struggling player might overthink things, Schwartz sounds like he doesn't want to overthink what's now going right.

"I'm gonna have to be here for a while to explain that all," he said Tuesday. "Just working, thinking less. We can get into that for another time (on) where I was earlier in the year."

Good health obviously has something to do with it. He missed a couple of October games after taking a puck off the foot/leg. And then missed 11 more contests in November and early December with what was variously described as a wrist/hand/finger injury.

But Schwartz also added: "I think confidence in any sport is huge for your mindset and how you feel going into the game."

Schwartz's confidence had to take a quantum leap with that Game 5 score against Winnipeg. Beginning with that goal, he has scored all 12 of his postseason goals in the Blues' last 15 games.

"I honestly think that (goal) definitely got his confidence back, for sure," Edmundson said. "Just that line in general has been playing unbelievable. So we've been feeding off them."

Schwartz was reunited with his friend and fellow Saskatchewan native Brayden Schenn late in that Winnipeg game.

Late in the Round 2 series against Dallas, Berube put the old band completely back together, adding Vladimir Tarasenko to the line with Schwartz and Schenn. Members of that line have scored nine goals with nine assists in the eight games since being reformed.

"Obviously, we've seen that going back a year, two years," Berube said. "If you remember 30 games in (last season), they were one of the best lines in the National Hockey League. They've been really good at times going forward and putting it all together, and they're definitely doing a good job now.

"They're working hard together, and when they're working hard together and they're doing things together out there — connected — they're a real good line."

Berube would like four more wins' worth of play like that.

Then, and only then, it could be time once again for Mexico. ∎

Pat Maroon and David Perron congratulate Jaden Schwartz during the Western Conference Final against the San Jose Sharks.

ST. LOUIS POST-DISPATCH

TUESDAY • 05.28.2019 • $2.50

GAME 1

4  2

BOSTON LEADS SERIES 1-0

GIVEAWAY

Turnovers, bad penalties cost Blues 2-0 lead

Bruins fourth-line forward Sean Kuraly scores the winning goal past Blues defender Joel Edmundson and goalie Jordan Binnington on Monday in Game 1 of the Stanley Cup Final.

GAME 1 Mon. at Boston	GAME 2 Wed. at Boston	GAME 3 7 p.m. Saturday at Blues NBCSN
Bos 0 2 2 — 4	Bos 2 0 0 0 — 2	
StL 1 1 0 — 2	StL 0 1 1 — 2	
GWG: Kuraly		

Subscribe for every cold, icy...

TODAY'S COMPLETE NEWSPAPER I...

VOL 141, No J45 ©2019

ST. LOUIS POST-DISPATCH

THURSDAY • 05.30.2019 • $2.50

GAME 2

3  2

SERIES TIED 1-1

FINALS FIRST!

OT win is first title-series victory in Blues history

The Blues celebrate after Carl Gunnarsson scored in overtime of Game 2 of the Stanley Cup Final to beat Boston on Wednesday. The franchise had been 0-12 in Stanley Cup Final games.

J.B. FORBES • jforbes@post-dispatch.com

GAME 1 Mon. at Boston	GAME 2 Wed. at Boston	GAME 3 7 p.m. Saturday at Blues NBCSN	GAME 4 7 p.m. Monday at Blues	GAME 5 7 p.m. Thursday 6/6 at Boston KSDK (Ch.5)	GAME 6* 7 p.m. Sunday 6/9 at Blues KSDK (Ch.5)	GAME 7* 7 p.m. Wednesday 6/12 at Boston KSDK (Ch.5)
Bos 0 2 2 — 4	Bos 2 0 0 0 — 2					
StL 1 1 0 — 2	StL 0 1 1 — 2					
GWG: Kuraly	GWG: Gunnarsson			* IF NECESSARY		

Subscribe for every cold, icy detail at STLtoday.com/subscribenow

TODAY'S COMPLETE NEWSPAPER INSIDE STANLEY CUP FINAL EDITION

VOL 141, No J52 ©2019   1   M

SUNDAY POST-DISPATCH

SUNDAY • 06.02.2019 • $4.00 • FINAL EDITION

GAME 3

7  2

BOSTON LEADS SERIES 2-1

UPENDED

Dominant Bruins score 4 power-play goals

Blues forward Brayden Schenn flips through the air next to Boston's David Pastrnak early in Game 3 of the Stanley Cup Final on Saturday at Enterprise Center.

J.B. FORBES • jforbes@post-dispatch.com

GAME 1 Mon. at Boston	GAME 2 Wed. at Boston	GAME 3 Sat. at Blues	GAME 4 7 p.m. Monday at Blues	GAME 5 7 p.m. Thursday at Boston KSDK (Ch.5)	GAME 6* 7 p.m. Sunday 6/9 at Blues KSDK (Ch.5)	GAME 7* 7 p.m. Wednesday 6/12 at Boston KSDK (Ch.5)
Bos 0 2 2 — 4	Bos 2 0 0 1 — 3	Bos 3 2 2 — 7				
StL 1 1 0 — 2	StL 0 1 1 — 2	StL 0 1 1 — 2				
GWG: Kuraly	GWG: Gunnarsson	GWG: Kuraly		* IF NECESSARY		

Subscribe for every cold, icy detail at STLtoday.com/subscribenow

TODAY'S COMPLETE NEWSPAPER INSIDE STANLEY CUP FINAL EDITION

VOL 141, No J53 ©2019   2   M

ST. LOUIS POST-DISPATCH

TUESDAY • 06.04.2019 • $2.50

GAME 4

4  2

SERIES TIED 2-2

OH, REALLY!

Blues tie series behind O'Reilly's two goals

Blues center Ryan O'Reilly (90) celebrates his first-period goal Monday, about two hours before his third-period score was the winning goal in Game 4 of the Stanley Cup Final.

LAURIE SKRIVAN • lskrivan@post-dispatch.com

GAME 1 5/27 at Boston	GAME 2 Wed. at Boston	GAME 3 Sat. at Blues	GAME 4 Mon. at Blues	GAME 5 7 p.m. Thursday at Boston KSDK (Ch.5)	GAME 6 7 p.m. Sunday at Blues KSDK (Ch.5)	GAME 7* 7 p.m. Wednesday 6/12 at Boston KSDK (Ch.5)
Bos 0 2 2 — 4	Bos 2 0 0 1 — 3	Bos 3 2 2 — 7	Bos 2 0 2 — 4			
StL 1 1 0 — 2	StL 0 1 1 — 2	StL 0 1 1 — 2	StL 1 1 0 — 2			
GWG: Kuraly	GWG: Gunnarsson	GWG: Kuraly	GWG: O'Reilly	* IF NECESSARY		

Subscribe for every cold, icy detail at STLtoday.com/subscribenow

TODAY'S COMPLETE NEWSPAPER INSIDE STANLEY CUP FINAL EDITION

VOL 141, No J55 ©2019   2   M

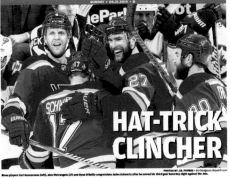

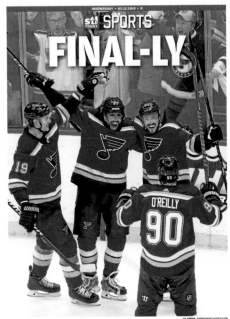

BLUES 2, JETS 1
APRIL 10, 2019 • WINNIPEG, MANITOBA

BETTER LATE THAN NEVER

BLUES JUMP OUT ON TOP OF JETS WITH RALLY IN FINAL PERIOD

BY JIM THOMAS

So this is what playoff hockey looks like. Hits. Mayhem. More hits. Ill will. Even more hits. Screaming. Booing. Cheering.

And then along came Tyler Bozak with the game-winning goal with just two minutes five seconds to play, giving the Blues a heart-pounding 2-1 victory over Winnipeg. Bozak turned the lights out on the Jets' Whiteout in the opening game of this Western Conference playoff series.

In the annals of Blues playoff history, it was the fourth-latest game-winning goal scored in regulation.

Better late than never, right?

During an otherwise highly successful regular season, the Blues were 2-23-6 when trailing after two periods. They picked a good time for No. 3, getting goals from David Perron and then Bozak to erase a 1-0 Jets lead at Bell MTS Place — one of the league's toughest venues on visiting teams.

"I had a lot of chances tonight, so I knew the puck was kind of following me around a bit," said Bozak, who led the Blues with six shots on goal, matching his season high. "It's always fun when that happens. So after the few I missed it was definitely nice to get one in there."

Oakville's Pat Maroon did the heavy lifting on the play, carrying the puck into the offensive zone despite some determined checking by Winnipeg, then winning a puck battle behind the net to set up Bozak.

"The D-man poached me and I tried to chip it over his stick," Maroon said. "Got with it, and there were three guys on my back there. I was just trying to find the puck in my feet and I got loose and Bozy was high slot.

"I seen him in the glare of my eye. ... Good shot."

Maroon played with a heavy heart because his grandfather, Ernest Ferrara, passed away the day before Game 1. His nickname was "Jocko" and he was 94. That's a long run, and a great nickname.

"He was behind me tonight. ... He was watching above," Maroon said. "Obviously that was for him. It's been emotional, tough days for me. Being with the guys and having them by my side has been really good."

Following Bozak's goal, the Blues still had to negotiate 125 seconds of harrying hockey against one of the NHL's most explosive scoring teams, including the last 100 seconds with Jets goalie Connor Hellebuyck pulled in favor of an extra attacker.

"The mindset was just compete to the end and give the team a chance to win," goalie Jordan Binnington said. "That buzzer couldn't have come sooner. We were just battling throughout in our D-zone. It was a grind right till the end. So it was a good win."

Just 34 seconds into the game, Jets star Mark Scheifele tried to take a bite out of Binnington, slamming into him behind the net as the Blues rookie tried to clear the puck.

"It's playoff hockey," Binnington said. "I can take a hit."

And with just 13 seconds left in the game, Binnington bit back, robbing Scheifele of what looked like the game-tying goal with the save of the night — sliding over from his left to right in the crease.

"They were moving the puck around," Binnington said. "It went down to Scheifele and I had to make a little bit of a desperation save there and hope for the best, with the boys coming and clearing out the rebound. That's all I remember."

Well, one other thing. He also remembers the booing.

From the opening faceoff — before it actually — it was the world against Binnington. Well, at least the corner of the world known as Manitoba.

During the week, there were comments from the Jets'

Robert Thomas (18) and Tyler Bozak (21) celebrate Bozak's goal against the Winnipeg Jets during the third period of Game 1.

locker room about how they wanted to make him nervous. Then there was the unearthing of culturally insensitive tweets made by Binnington six years ago — on the eve of Wednesday's playoff game, by a former Winnipeg resident.

Then came Scheifele's hit, which brought a two-minute minor for interference. Then came the booing. Loud booing e-v-e-r-y time Binnington touched the puck.

Asked if he'd ever been booed before, Binnington replied: "I don't think so. Yeah, they were all over me, but it's a part of the game. It's exciting. They're passionate. ... So whatever. We gotta handle it. Stay composed, so on to the next game."

The victory was a study in perseverance for the Blues, who were literally knocked off their game for most of the first two periods. This wasn't a case of Winnipeg's speed or firepower causing trouble. It was their physical play and hitting — 24 hits in the first two periods alone and 36 in the game.

"Obviously an exciting building," Bozak said. "The crowd was awesome. We were nervous at the start, but I thought we found our game as the game went on. I thought everyone did a great job."

Midway through the opening period there were only three shots on goal apiece for the teams. But as the frame wore on, Winnipeg started to get the best of the hitting and most of the offensive zone time.

It paid off for the Jets at the 13:28 mark of the period, when Patrik Laine — name sound familiar? — ripped a wicked wrist shot past Binnington from the slot. Laine, you may recall, tied a Blues' opponent record with five goals against St. Louis in an 8-4 victory at Enterprise Center on Nov. 24.

"Their goal gave them momentum a little bit and got the crowd into it even more," Perron said. "We just kept climbing, climbing, grinding. Our second intermission, I thought we were calm and composed in (the locker room). It was good to see."

Perron stopped the Winnipeg momentum with his game-tying goal off a drop pass from Colton Parayko at the 4:05 mark of the third. That seemed to get the Blues back on their game. By game's end, they had negated Winnipeg's home-ice advantage in the best-of-7 series.

"Well it's one win, but it's a good win for sure," interim coach Craig Berube said. "We come in here, this is a tough building and it's an excellent team over there. It's going to be a battle. We were on the right side tonight." ∎

St. Louis Blues goaltender Jordan Binnington stops a shot during the third period. Binnington had 24 saves and only allowed one goal in the win.

BLUES 4, JETS 3
APRIL 12, 2019 • WINNIPEG, MANITOBA

TAKING CONTROL

BLUES ARE HALFWAY HOME AFTER WINNING AGAIN IN WINNIPEG

BY JIM THOMAS

It's doubtful anyone saw this coming, not even the Blues. But they did it again Friday, outlasting the Winnipeg Jets for the second time in three days at Bell MTS Place.

This time it was 4-3, with Ryan O'Reilly providing the game-winner early in the third period. The Blues are now halfway home in their best-of-seven Western Conference playoff series, up two games to none as they head home for Games 3 and 4 at Enterprise Center.

"Coming into this barn, it's a hard barn to play," said Pat Maroon, who scored a key second-period goal just when it seemed like the game was slipping away from St. Louis. "But to take two is a really good sign for this team.

"But that doesn't mean anything. We gotta focus on Game 3 right now. We know they're gonna come hard. We gotta continue what we're doing."

The math now favors the Blues. Teams that have started 2-0 in Stanley Cup playoff series are 318-50 in terms of taking the series, an 86.4 percent success rate. But the math also says the Blues need two more wins before they can celebrate anything.

"This is a real good hockey team that we beat twice here — a really good hockey team — and they're going to give us their best game (in) Game 3 at home," interim coach Craig Berube said. "There's no reason to get too high. You've got to stay ready and we've got to play even better than we played."

This was a game of ebbs and flows, shifting momentum, big hits, and obviously a lot more offense than was on display in Game 1.

In the ebb-and-flow department, the Blues went without a shot for the last 10 minutes, 34 seconds of the first period, a stretch in which the Jets tied the game 1-all and seized momentum.

Then the Jets went silent for 13:34 of the second period, a stretch in which the Blues outshot them 12-0 and turned a 2-1 deficit into a 3-2 lead.

Then there was the revelation that is Oskar Sundqvist. He scored twice. Twice.

"He's just always in the right areas," Maroon said. "He's low-and-slow in the center. He's always open in the middle of the ice and he does a really good job of supporting the puck."

The revelation that is Jordan Binnington became only the fourth NHL goalie in the past 32 years to win each of his first two playoff road games. Binnington made 26 saves, and yes the Jets got him three times, but he never withered.

"They've had the chances, and Binner's been there to stop them," Joel Edmundson said. "He had another outstanding game tonight for the most part."

The Blues special teams were just short of a disaster area. After finishing 10th in the regular season in power-play efficiency, they went 0-for-4 Friday — and are now 0-for-7 in the series. And their ninth-ranked penalty kill unit allowed two goals to the Jets (one by Blues-killer Patrik Laine and one by Mark Scheifele).

"We've had some good (power-play) opportunities," O'Reilly said. "We have to maybe simplify a bit, maybe shoot pucks more. They're things that can dramatically affect the outcome, and it's something we're obviously going to take time, review it and get that sorted out."

Despite those glitches and others, when the Blues needed a response, they got one.

They played hurt: Robert Bortuzzo left the ice bleeding in the third period, apparently getting his wrist or hand cut, only to return and finish out the game. Berube said he would know more about Bortuzzo's injury after the team returned Saturday to St. Louis.

They absorbed hits: Like Sundqvist getting absolutely leveled by Adam Lowry. "It's a clean hit," Sundqvist said.

The Jets dished out 32 hits Friday, not all of them of the clean variety. But the Blues stayed disciplined and didn't try

The Blues celebrate a 4-3 win against the Winnipeg Jets in Game 2, giving them a 2-0 series lead.

to retaliate and thus risk penalties, apparently to the chagrin of the Jets.

"It's kind of frustrating them," Edmundson said. "There's some chirping going on between the benches, and I think it's getting underneath their skin a bit. You can definitely see it on their faces. It's fun to watch.

"I'm not the one to chirp out there, but we gotta couple guys that are good at it. We're just trying to play smart hockey."

When all was said and done, the Blues persevered once again, pulling the plug on the white noise of the Whiteout at Bell MTS. The building was oh-so-quiet at game's end.

"Our motto in here is not get too low, not get too high," Edmundson said. "So it doesn't matter if we're down a goal or up a goal, we're even-keel and we're just going out there, we're sticking to our system. And I think we've been doing that for 60 minutes both games."

Despite occasional outbursts of offensive prowess by Winnipeg, the Blues frustrated the Jets at times and kept their shot total relatively low.

After O'Reilly's first playoff goal since the 2013-14 season gave the Blues their 4-3 lead less than four minutes into the third period, they once again were able to keep Winnipeg off the scoreboard down the stretch.

The Blues have owned the third period here, outscoring the Jets 3-0 combined in both games. Otherwise, they don't pull out a pair of one-goal victories. How have they done it?

"Just grinding 'em down low," Maroon said. "Getting to our game, which is getting pucks deep. Just wearing their 'D' down and trying to get second and third opportunities. That fourth goal there, (Jay) Bouwmeester made a heckuva play, great breakout (pass)."

O'Reilly did the rest. He beat Jets goalie Connor Hellebuyck far side from a relatively long distance. It was one of those shots that leaves you wondering: How did that get through? It looked like O'Reilly used a Winnipeg defender to screen Hellebuyck.

"I think lots of times you practice that — of shooting through something," O'Reilly said. "It's obviously a great pass by Bouw, kind of put me in there in a good spot. And I'm just trying to get through on to the net. It was obviously a big play that was nice to have."

So now, after surviving two games worth of Jets-mania in one of the most intimidating buildings in the NHL, it's on to Enterprise.

"I think it's gonna be louder than this," Edmundson said. "I'm expecting an unreal crowd. They've been supporting us all year, so I know they're really looking forward to Games 3 and 4."

Which sounds like a safe bet. ■

Oskar Sundqvist scores against Winnipeg Jets goaltender Connor Hellebuyck during the first period of the 4-3 win. Sundqvist had two goals in the game.

JETS 6, BLUES 3
APRIL 14, 2019 • ST. LOUIS, MISSOURI

RUDE AWAKENING

BLUES WARBLE A SOUR NOTE AS JETS CLIMB BACK INTO SERIES

BY JIM THOMAS

We now have a series. And we now know the Blues and the series are going back to Winnipeg.

With an opportunity to put their foot on the collective throat of the Jets and go up 3-0 in the matchup, the Blues got outworked, outhit, outshot — and most importantly, outscored in a 6-3 loss.

The Blues still lead their best-of-seven Western Conference first-round playoff series, now two games to one, but they'll have to play much better than they did Sunday at Enterprise Center to avoid having this series go to Winnipeg tied 2-2.

"There's no panic here," said Vladimir Tarasenko, who scored one of the Blues' two power play goals Sunday night. "Nobody said it was going to be easy. We'll be ready for our next game (on Tuesday night) and come out to win the game."

David Perron, who scored the Blues' other power play goal, was reading off the same script.

"There's no panic in here," Perron said. "We've just got to look at some video, talk about things (Monday). We'll be fine. It's one game. Whether you win 7-0 or you lose 1-0, it's worth one right now. Got to give them credit, they played a good game."

After the morning skate, Winnipeg forward Blake Wheeler was asked how the Jets could solve the rock that was rookie goalie Jordan Binnington.

"The last thing we're worried about is offense," Wheeler said. "We're going to score. We always have. We've got to try to limit the amount we're giving up and make it really tough for these guys to create offense. When we get our looks, we'll bury them."

He was right on all counts.

Binnington kept the Blues in the game with an amazing first period. But the Jets kept pounding on the rock and broke through with six goals — scoring three in the second period and three in the third.

Kyle Connor got Binnington twice. Blues nemesis Patrik

Laine scored his third goal in as many games in this series. Kevin Hayes, Brandon Tanev, and Dustin Byfuglien also contributed to the Jets' six-pack.

In three games at Enterprise this season, the Jets are 3-0 and have outscored the Blues by a combined 19-8.

In four games at Bell MTS Place over the regular and postseason, the Blues are 3-0-1 with three one-goal victories, plus an overtime loss.

As for Sunday's six goals, that's by far the most allowed by Binnington in his young NHL career. He had not allowed more than three goals in any prior game at home and had not given up more than four goals in any game during his amazing season.

That changed Sunday, but Blues interim coach Craig Berube remained firmly in Binnington's corner after a game in which the Jets were outshooting the Blues 23-8 at one point in the second period.

"It could've been 4-0 in the first period, so he played a pretty good game," Berube said.

Almost from the moment they went up two games to none with Friday's 4-3 victory in Winnipeg, the Blues talked about how they expected the Jets to push hard from the start of Game 3. But from the opening faceoff Sunday, they didn't act like it. They seemed almost unprepared for what Winnipeg threw at them.

"From the start of the game, we weren't really where we needed to be," Alex Pietrangelo said. "We didn't really manage the game the way we wanted to."

On defense, the Blues seemed to be chasing more often than not.

On offense, the Blues got next to no time in the Winnipeg zone until the third period.

"We gotta get the puck deep," Berube said. "That's our game. Moving the puck quick, getting it in the offensive zone, working the team down low in the offensive zone. That's our game.

Blues goalie Jordan Binnington can't stop the shot by Patrik Laine for the Jets' second goal during the second period of Game 3.

"We're a north team and we didn't go north tonight."

There can be no disputing that because their entire game went south.

"Tonight was not really our team, obviously," Perron said. "We weren't happy with our effort."

That was true right from the start. It seemed as if the Jets were on the power play for the first eight minutes or so of the game. And then they were actually on one, with Joel Edmundson sent off for tripping Laine at the 8:47 mark. There was a point in the period when Winnipeg had an 11-2 advantage in shots on goal.

But for the time being the Jets couldn't solve Binnington. He made several tough stops but the signature save came when Mathieu Perreault seemingly had the goalie dead to rights skating in on left wing. But Binnington got the top of his stick on the puck and deflected it away.

As Perreault skated to the Winnipeg bench seconds later, he lifted an arm in the air in exasperation.

The Jets kept firing, and finally got to Binnington with

three goals in a span of 4:01 in the second period. With the Blues up 1-0 on Perron's first-period goal, Hayes tied the game with a shot that deflected in off the stick of Pietrangelo.

Hayes' shot typified Winnipeg's approach to a large degree — when all else failed, the Jets simply sent to puck toward the net hoping something good would come of it. Something good came out of it six times.

In contrast to Winnipeg, the Blues were too fine in their shot selection for much of the first two periods, looking for the perfect shot — or at least a better shot. So much so that the Blues heard boos — yes, boos — from the fans on a power-play opportunity late in the second period when they took their time getting the puck up the ice and then passed, passed, and passed some more.

Tarasenko's first goal of the series briefly made it a game again early in the third period, narrowing Winnipeg's lead to 3-2. But then came three more Winnipeg goals that — to borrow Wheeler's term — buried the Blues.

And made it a series. ◼

JETS 2, BLUES 1 (OT)
APRIL 16, 2019 • ST. LOUIS, MISSOURI

BACK TO EVEN

HEARTBREAK IN OVERTIME AS BLUES FALL AT HOME AGAIN

BY JIM THOMAS

The Blues got where they are this season by winning the close ones, nearly all of them down the stretch. Starting with the third game of the franchise-record 11-game winning streak — a 3-2 win Feb. 5 at Florida — the Blues were 12-0-4 in games decided by one goal.

Included in that total were 2-1 and 4-3 victories in Winnipeg to start this Western Conference quarterfinal series. The one-goal mojo changed Tuesday in heartbreaking fashion at Enterprise Center.

On what Winnipeg coach Paul Maurice called a "special night" for Blues goalie Jordan Binnington, Kyle Connor scored the game-winner 6 minutes 2 seconds into overtime, giving the Jets a 2-1 victory and tying the best-of-seven series at two games apiece.

"It's frustrating," Blues captain Alex Pietrangelo said. "We knew it was going to be a hard series, right? We took two in their building, so regroup and hopefully steal another one in there."

For the Blues, the anticipated hard series got harder after Tuesday's contest before 18,346 at Enterprise center.

"It's the best out of three," interim coach Craig Berube said. "We won there twice and we have confidence there, and will have confidence next game."

The victory allowed Winnipeg to regain home ice advantage in the series, not that that means anything. The home team has yet to win so far, and if you take it back to the regular season, the Jets are 4-0 in Enterprise and the Blues are 3-0-1 at Bell MTS.

"It's strange," Binnington said, speaking of the home ice disadvantage. "Hopefully we win again in Winnipeg. I don't know, I don't have an explanation for it. It's just the way it's going."

Binnington lost back-to-back games for the first time in his storybook rookie season, even though it was among his best performances yet. His record in net was 24-6-1 overall —

including regular-season and playoff results — entering Tuesday's Game 4. And he was 6-0 following his previous six losses.

"He played a great game," Berube said.

And that was putting it mildly.

Binnington stopped 37 of 39 shots Tuesday and had no chance on either Winnipeg goal — a game-tying score by Mark Scheifele at the 7:33 mark of the third period, and Connor's game-winner. He stopped rushes and breakaways, point blank shots, and had Brandon Tanev slamming his stick on the ice after his backhand breakaway attempt sailed high and may have grazed the crossbar midway through the second period.

After two scoreless periods of intense and highly-entertaining hockey, the Blues tilted the game in their favor on Vladimir Tarasenko's second power play goal in as many games. He took a pass from Pietrangelo at the left faceoff circle — one of his favorite spots on the ice — and zipped a shot past Jets goalie Connor Hellebuyck to break a scoreless tie just 35 seconds into the third period.

The Blues had the next two shots of the period, but the Jets then slowly but convincingly took control. They outshot the Blues 15-4 over the final 16:48 of regulation, and 5-1 in overtime.

"Just a little passive, defensive," Pietrangelo said. "I think we're better when we're aggressive."

The push was very noticeable after the Scheifele goal, which came on an all-out charge to the net. He took a pinpoint pass from Connor, and at full speed tipped the puck past Binnington, bowling over the Blues' goalie with enough force that it knocked Binnington's stick away.

Less than a minute and a half earlier, chants of "Binn-ing-ton! Binn-ing-ton! Binn-ing-ton!" cascaded from the rafters at Enterprise after another show-stopping save. This came after a shot by Scheifele appeared to get caught up in Binnington's mask and it looked like the goalie spit the puck out of his mask.

Jordan Binnington keeps an eye on the loose puck, stopping Winnipeg's Adam Lowry from scoring during the second period of the Game 4 overtime loss.

"That was a pretty cool moment obviously, but I'd rather win," Binnington said.

And then the Scheifele goal changed everything, tilting the game back Winnipeg's way.

"Any time you get a goal, there's momentum," Berube said. "You gotta answer back. They were obviously excited about that goal. Nice goal. And they had momentum after that for a bit."

Well, for more than a bit. Even so, the Blues did have a late chance to end the game in regulation when Mathieu Perreault was called for tripping Vince Dunn with 3:41 to play. It was Perreault's cross-checking penalty against Pietrangelo that led to the Tarasenko power play goal at the start of the third.

The Blues didn't get much done on the late power play — it looked predictable and passive.

"We only had the one look really," Berube said. "But we could've attacked more on that power play and did a better job. But it just didn't happen."

Pat Maroon, arguably the Blues' best forward Tuesday, had two chances trying to jam the puck past Hellebuyck. But that was it for that power play.

As was the case for much of the third period, Winnipeg controlled the play in overtime leading up to Connor's game-winner — his third goal in the last two games.

"We got caught with three guys on the forecheck," Berube said. "(Brayden) Schenn was on (Dustin) Byfuglien and they were battling for the puck, and Byfuglien won that battle and got it up to their forwards.

"Looked like (Colton) Parayko just got caught pivoting the wrong way and they came back and made a play."

Blake Wheeler carried the puck on the rush, with Parayko defending. There was a shot by Scheifele and then the game-winner by Connor. A huge play for the Jets and enormous disappointment for the Blues.

"That was a hard-fought battle," Scheifele said. "St. Louis played hard all night. 'Wheels' made a great play driving the net and I kind of tried to stiff one far side. Binnington made another big save, like he did all night. I got (the rebound), and saw (Connor) wide open in front, and he got it and batted it in." ▪

BLUES 3, JETS 2
APRIL 18, 2019 • WINNIPEG, MANITOBA

THURSDAY NIGHT MIRACLE

BLUES SCORE WITH 15 SECONDS LEFT TO STUN JETS

BY JIM THOMAS

By now the strategy is crystal clear for the Blues. They should simply forfeit Game 6 Saturday in St. Louis, proceed directly to Game 7 here, clinch the series, and move on to Round 2 of Lord Stanley's playoffs.

Because apparently it no longer is possible for the Blues to lose at Bell MTS Place. They were down 2-0 in the first period Thursday. On the ropes when they had to kill a four-minute high-sticking penalty to Robert Thomas. Within inches of trailing 3-0 when Colton Parayko fell on Kevin Hayes and Hayes' own stick redirected the dribbling puck away from the goal line.

A game-tying goal by Brayden Schenn — moved down to the second line — came with 6 minutes 8 seconds to play in the game. And then the game-winner by Jaden Schwartz with 15 seconds to play. It all added up to a spellbinding 3-2 victory. If the Blues manage to close out this series, it will be a game talked about for years in team lore.

Up 3-2 in this best-of-seven series, the Blues can send Winnipeg packing with a victory Saturday at Enterprise Center. But that will require a home victory — something that has not happened yet in this series by either team.

Can the Blues make it happen in Game 6?

"Well, that's what we're hoping to do," interim coach Craig Berube said, smiling broadly. "I guess we'll have to wait and see."

Jets goalie Connor Hellebuyck wasn't a big fan of the Schwartz goal, his first of the series and second game-winner of the season.

"Lucky pinballs," Hellebuyck said. "The puck just bounced and ended up right on their tape. Tough to eat that one, but I thought we were the better team. If we keep fighting here, it's not over."

Your thoughts, Alex Pietrangelo?

"They can say that all they want," Pietrangelo said.

"Their first one's a lucky bounce, too. He just throws the puck from the corner without looking and it goes right on the guy's tape. They can make all the excuses they want but we found a way to score."

Lucky or not, Schwartz said it was the biggest goal of his career so far.

"I've got to say yes," Schwartz said. "At this point and time in the series, and with that much time left, with the chance to go home and close it out, it's big. But, you know how the home games have gone. We've got to regroup and be ready."

The home games haven't gone good for either team. With Thursday's victory, the Blues have won all three games in this Western Conference quarterfinal at one of the NHL's toughest venues. And four in a row overall if you go back to a 1-0 victory Dec. 7.

But the Jets have won both series games in St. Louis and are 4-0 overall at Enterprise if you include the regular season.

It sure looked like the trend would end Thursday. Just moments after the completion of "O Canada," it was "Oh, boy" for the Blues.

Brandon Tanev's shot from basically the goal line appeared to hit the side of the net and caromed right to Adam Lowry in the slot. The St. Louis native wasted no time sending a shot past Jordan Binnington for a goal just 12 seconds into the game — the fastest playoff goal allowed by the Blues in team history.

Shortly after that goal, Carl Gunnarsson — back in the lineup in place of Robert Bortuzzo — was moved up to the team's top defensive pairing with Pietrangelo. Vince Dunn joined Joel Edmundson on the third pairing.

A one-goal deficit was one thing. But a two-goal Jets lead was something else. And it became 2-0 with 6:25 to play in the

Carl Gunnarsson (4), Jaden Schwartz (17), Alexander Steen (20), and Tyler Bozak (21) celebrate Schwartz's go-ahead goal against the Jets in the final minute of Game 5.

opening period when Kevin Hayes dashed down right wing and around Edmundson. Hayes cut in front of Binnington, who stopped the attempted jam shot.

On the rebound attempt, Ivan Barbashev stuck a stick out, but didn't get a body on Hayes, who was able to stuff home the rebound.

Chants of "You look nervous! You look nervous!" rang out — a reference to Binnington's "Do I look nervous?" comment after a 2-0 victory over Nashville on Feb. 26.

Binnington heard the chants.

"Yeah, that's incredible," he said. "You get what you ask for because when I was younger, I really enjoyed that stuff and always wanted it. And now it's here. It doesn't feel as good as I thought, but it's cool, it's really cool."

As if in defiance of those chants, Binnington stayed cool the reminder of the game. He stopped a few breakaways, got some huge help from Parayko on the near-goal by Hayes, and avoided losing a third consecutive game for the first time in his young NHL career.

"My job is to give the team a chance to win," Binnington said. "Obviously (Winnipeg) got out to an early lead and I kind of had to shut the door from there on out. It wasn't easy and the boys really helped me out and battled. The penalty kill was outstanding, and it was a great team effort for pretty much 60 minutes."

The work of the PK unit was stellar on the double-minor against Thomas.

"Probably the difference in the game," Berube said.

Maybe. Or maybe it was another lineup shuffle by Berube, moving the struggling Schenn down to the second line and David Perron up to the first line.

Ryan O'Reilly got the Blues on the board with a power-play goal at the start of the third period and then Schenn and Schwartz went to work to help carve out a slice of Blues history.

"We're just staying with it," Schwartz said.

"We believe in each other, we believe in the system and we work as a team."

And they're just one victory away from Round 2. ■

Brayden Schenn (10) scores the tying goal against Winnipeg goaltender Connor Hellebuyck during the third period of the dramatic 3-2 victory.

BLUES 3, JETS 2
APRIL 20, 2019 ● ST. LOUIS, MISSOURI

HAT-TRICK CLINCHER

BLUES ELIMINATE JETS TO ADVANCE

BY JIM THOMAS

You could say it took Jaden Schwartz 87 games to get going — that would be 82 regular-season games and five postseason affairs. Fair enough. But when he got going?

Well, hats off to Schwartz. Lots of them.

"I wasn't really looking at the hats," Schwartz said. "I was just trying to catch my breath. And we were trying to get the faceoff there and they kept throwing them. It was slowing the game down a bit."

Fans will be fans.

As if his game-winner with 15 seconds left in Game 5 Thursday wasn't enough, Schwartz scored a natural hat trick Saturday — the first three goals of the game, in fact, and what turned out to be all three Blues goals in a 3-2 series-clinching victory over Winnipeg at Enterprise Center.

The Jets and goalie Connor Hellebuyck can't complain about "pinball bounces" in this one. Well, maybe they can.

"You can't get any luckier than that," Hellebuyck said afterwards. "What I saw was a puck that hit the side of the net or the post, one of the two, and somehow it jumped straight up and (hit) crossbar, off my back. If that's not the fortunate bounce that you consider luck, then I don't know what is."

He was describing Schwartz's first goal, which came just 23 seconds into the game. Schwartz saw it at least a little differently.

"It just went off the post, and I was kind of in the right spot, right time," Schwartz said. "Bounced on my stick. (The puck) was underneath him a little bit but I had room."

Schwartz scored a power-play goal with 7:24 left in the second period to make it 2-0 Blues and got his third early in the third finishing off a rush with Brayden Schenn. Throw in his goal with 15 seconds remaining Thursday to stun Winnipeg 3-2 and Schwartz has scored the last four Blues goals.

"What a boss," goalie Jordan Binnington said. "He's playing great, and the (playoff) beard looks pretty good on him too."

Winnipeg made it just a tad too interesting in the third period with a goal by Dustin Byfuglien with 7:34 to play and one by Bryan Little with 37 seconds left.

"It got a little tighter than we wanted, that's for sure," interim coach Craig Berube said. "I'll tell you that. But 50 minutes or more we were pretty dominant."

All season long, the Blues have made history, reached milestones, done things rarely achieved in team and NHL annals. From their worst-to-(playoff) berth finish, from the accomplishments of Binnington, to that 11-game winning streak.

But they did not want to be part of the first NHL playoff series in which the road team won the first six games. So with Saturday's victory, the Blues made no history. They did, however, clinch the best-of-seven Western Conference quarterfinal 4-2, sending the high-flying Jets into the offseason.

The Blues will play Dallas or Nashville in the next round. With a 5-3 victory Saturday over Nashville, Dallas leads that series 3-2. The Blues get home ice advantage if their opponent is Dallas; if it's Nashville, the Predators get home ice.

The Jets may disagree, but it seemed obvious the third-period comeback by the Blues on Thursday — three unanswered goals in the period including Schwartz's stunner at the end — took something out of Winnipeg.

There seemed to be a definite carryover effect to that game, in terms of the Blues' domination.

"We talked about bringing that momentum from the third period of Game 5," Berube said. "And I think that the guys did. We mentioned it (Friday). Talked today about it. We had good energy and played hard."

The Jets scored just 12 seconds into Game 5. The Blues couldn't match that Saturday — they had to settle for 23 seconds. Schenn, centering the second line as he did for the final two periods Thursday, charged down right wing, cut sharply to the net and fired on Hellebuyck.

Blues goalie Jordan Binnington shakes hands with Jets goalie Connor Hellebuyck after St. Louis eliminated Winnipeg from the playoffs with a 3-2 win.

Schwartz swooped in backdoor, to score the second-fastest goal of the season for St. Louis. Ryan O'Reilly scored 18 seconds in, way back on Oct. 27 in Chicago.

And it was the third-quickest goal in Blues playoff history. Only Sergio Momesso (18 seconds in 1990) and Brett Hull (20 seconds in 1995) have done it quicker in the postseason.

Spurred on by the goal and a jacked-up crowd of 18,524 at Enterprise, this easily was the Blues' strongest first period of the series. St. Louis had a 11-5 advantage in shots on goal and a whopping 20-8 edge in hits.

The Blues were even sharper in the second period. They were skating, shooting, controlling the play with tons of offensive zone time. They dominated, pure and simple.

The Blues outshot Winnipeg 16-1 in the second period.

"I think they missed one (shot)," Binnington said, referring to the statisticians. "I did my best to try to give my team a chance to win, they were playing so good. Just feed off the team's momentum, play the puck a little bit and do what I need to do to stay in it."

Perhaps there will be a statistical change later, but the official NHL postgame boxscore still showed the Jets with just one shot on goal in the period, which if it holds, is a St. Louis playoff record.

After two periods the Blues had outshot the Jets 27-6. The heralded Winnipeg top line of Kyle Connor, Mark Scheifele and Blake Wheeler — which had outplayed its St. Louis counterpart for large chunks of the series — was skunked. No goals, no assists.

"That's exactly what we wanted to do," Alex Pietrangelo said. "We wanted to be hard on their top line, come out strong. Got a lot of energy after that first shift. That's a heck of an effort all-around."

After Schwartz's third goal, derisive chants of "You look nervous!" rang out in Enterprise. They weren't directed at Binnington.

"The city's got my back, I guess," Binnington said. "That was pretty cool to see. The city's a great hockey town and sports town." ∎

Teammates congratulate Jaden Schwartz (17) after he scored his third goal for a hat trick during the series-clinching win over the Jets.

BLUES 3, STARS 2
APRIL 25, 2019 • ST. LOUIS, MISSOURI

ON THE RIGHT NOTE

HOT START FOR BLUES AND TARASENKO IN OPENING WIN OVER STARS

BY JIM THOMAS

Vladimir Tarasenko didn't feel like expounding on his exploits in Thursday's 3-2 victory over the Dallas Stars.

"I don't want to talk about this," Tarasenko said. "It's just the first game. We have a lot of hockey to play. I don't think it's right to talk about your moments in the game. It's just Game 1 and we have a win — it's the most exciting thing."

True, going up 1-0 in their best-of-seven Western Conference semifinal series with the Stars was exciting for the Blues and the 18,014 watching at Enterprise Center.

But Tarasenko was responsible for some exciting things himself, particularly a power play goal late in the second period, and what proved to be the game-winner on a mad dash to the net early in the third.

And despite his reticence to elaborate, there were plenty of others willing to talk up Tarasenko.

"He's just so strong," Vince Dunn said. "When he gets a step on you, it's hard to stop him."

Talented Dallas rookie Miro Heiskanen found this out the hard way early in the third period. Tarasenko charged down right wing with Heiskanen defending.

Tarasenko hesitated just inside the blue line, then hit full stride before cutting sharply to the net and beating Stars goalie Ben Bishop with a roof shot to the far side. That made it a 3-1 game.

"That was a massive play obviously with their pressure, and Vladi stepping up and making a huge play to give us some cushion there," Ryan O'Reilly said.

Tarasenko had tried the same move late in the second period. But on that one, he didn't quite get the angle and crashed into the side of the net as his wrister went wide.

Nonetheless, something good came out of it for St. Louis because Dallas defenseman (and former Blue) Roman Polak was whistled for hooking on the play at the 17:55 mark. A mere eight seconds into the power play, Tarasenko beat Bishop from the left faceoff circle.

"He has probably the best snap shot in the game — it's quick and a good shot there," said Bishop, also a former Blue as well as a Chaminade High product. "Would've liked to have that one back. ... He's a dangerous player, a good player, and you can see why."

Over the course of the season, Craig Berube has talked frequently with his players — Tarasenko included — about the need to drive the puck wide to the net with speed. It paid off Thursday.

How does he do that?

"Tarasenko? Just God-given talent," Berube said. "He's a powerful guy that can skate. When he drives wide like that, he's really tough to handle for a lot of people."

For Tarasenko, the two goals gave him nine points (five goals, four assists) in eight career playoff games against the Stars. In the regular season, he has 16 goals in 27 career games against Dallas, including three during the just-completed regular season.

So yes, he likes to see Stars. His second goal Thursday gave the Blues a cushion they needed because Blues nemesis Jamie Benn made it a 3-2 game with 2:17 to play. It looked like Binnington had smothered the puck with a snow-angel move but then all of a sudden there was Benn flipping it into the net for his sixth goal of this season (regular-season plus playoffs) against the Blues.

The Blues argued to no avail that the whistle had blown.

"I haven't re-watched it so I don't know what happened," Binnington said afterwards. "I snow-angeled it and hoped for the best but it went in. That's where we're at."

Both Binnington and Berube said the whistle had blown, but the NHL situation room in Toronto said it was informed by referees Chris Rooney and Gord Dwyer that the puck had completely crossed the goal line before they whistled the play dead.

Blues Robby Fabbri (15) and Ivan Barbashev (49) celebrate after Fabbri scored the first goal of the Game 1 win.

"It's the game of hockey," Binnington said. "You have to handle it and I think we handled it well."

It made for another tense finish, and yet another one-goal game for the Blues. But as Binnington said, they handled it. Again.

All five of their victories this postseason have been one-goal affairs. And since a 3-2 comeback win over the Florida Panthers on Feb. 5, the team is 16-1-4 in one-goal games.

Berube said to look for more of the same before this series is decided.

"It's tight out there," he said. "It's tough hockey, physical hockey. There were some big hits tonight. ... It's gonna be a tight series. What you saw tonight is what you're gonna see."

So the Blues began Round 2 of the Stanley Cup playoffs like they finished Round 1 five days ago — with a home victory.

Dallas gave the Blues trouble during the regular season, winning three of four, and had won six of seven overall dating back to the 2017-18 season. But Thursday was different, and not just because Robby Fabbri got the scoring going with his first goal since Nov. 23 against Nashville — the day after Thanksgiving.

Binnington became the first Blues rookie goaltender to win five games in one postseason and was sharp enough to receive more chants of "Binn-ing-ton! Binn-ing-ton!" from the sellout crowd. One of his best saves came with speedy Roope Hintz bearing down on left wing. Binnington made the save, losing his stick in the process.

"I think it was a little desperation play," Binnington said. "So it was kind of a 'yard sale' and just do whatever you can to stop the puck and it worked out there."

It was one of 16 saves made by Binnington in the period.

A few minutes later, Dallas' Blake Comeau raced in for a free puck with Dunn right with him. Binnington came out to get the puck and Comeau slammed into the Blues goalie, knocking him to the ice.

Dunn didn't like seeing his goaltender roughed up and went right after Comeau. Others joined. The night's best scrum resulted in penalties for Dunn and Alex Pietrangelo of the Blues. And Comeau and Esa Lindell of the Stars.

Berube thought the contact by Comeau could have been avoided and liked the response from his team.

"It could've been avoided for sure," Berube said. "Our guys, they're gonna protect their teammates. Unfortunately, we didn't get a power play out of it, which I think we should've."

The result of all that shoving, and some punching, was 5-on-5 skating. But as was the case when Mark Scheifele ran over Binnington in Game 1 of the Winnipeg series — Binnington can take a hit.

His words if you recall. Not ours. ∎

Vladimir Tarasenko celebrates with teammates Vince Dunn (left) and David Perron after scoring his second goal of the night.

STARS 4, BLUES 2
APRIL 27, 2019 • ST. LOUIS, MISSOURI

STARSTRUCK

DALLAS DOMINATES THE BLUES EARLY AND LATE TO TIE THE SERIES

BY JIM THOMAS

Even though they took Game 1, the Blues knew they had to be better managing the puck. They knew they had to start quicker. Neither happened Saturday, and this time they paid for their transgressions.

With the Blues looking a step slow early, Dallas had a 5-1 edge in shots just 2½ minutes into play. Getting the puck out of their zone again was an adventure early.

And by the end of first period they were in a 3-1 hole, a hole they couldn't climb out of in a 4-2 loss to the Stars before 18,285 at Enterprise Center.

"Obviously, you never want to give up three in a period," defenseman Colton Parayko said. "I thought we did a good job of sticking with it throughout the game. We had a good second-half push. They played well, too. So that's playoff hockey."

Playoff hockey that now has this Western Conference semifinal tied at 1-1, with the action shifting to Dallas for games Monday and Wednesday. The Blues need to be more aggressive at the start in those games if they want to take control of the series.

"They took advantage of some opportunities they had there," forward Jaden Schwartz said, speaking of the slow start Saturday. "Our puck play wasn't as good, wasn't as sharp as it usually is. ... We did a good job climbing back, but that's a lapse we can't have."

Schwartz's fifth goal of the playoffs and first of this series made it a 3-2 game early in the third period. But over the next 13½ minutes of play, the Blues were outshot 16-4. Not exactly what you'd call a third-period push.

The Stars peppered newly named Calder Trophy finalist Jordan Binnington with nine shots — on one two-minute power play — during that stretch, squeezing away any momentum the Blues hoped to muster after the Schwartz goal.

"I thought we were going real well," interim coach Craig Berube said. "We gave them that power play, they got momentum off it and they got some good looks and some shots. Binner made some real good saves there and kept us in it."

The power play came when David Perron was whistled for goaltender interference, a call that drew loud boos from the crowd. There was a lot of jostling going on in front of the net on the play, and Perron got caught shoving back at Stars netminder Ben Bishop.

Berube didn't like the call.

"Not really, no," he said. "Little bit of a dive by Bishop in my opinion."

After facing 17 shots in the third period in Game 1 Thursday, when the Blues were able to hold on for a 3-2 victory, Binnington faced 18 in the third period Saturday when the Blues were trying to mount a comeback. Not exactly a recipe for success.

Nor was going 0 for 5 on the power play, as was the case Saturday. The Blues were able to mount just eight shots combined on those five power plays — which included 24 seconds of 5-on-3 play in the first period. Or one less shot than Dallas had on that Perron infraction.

"We had some good looks," Schwartz said. "Obviously 'Bish' made some good saves. We hit some sticks and couldn't seem to get the bounce on our stick at the right time."

Over their previous five postseason games, dating back to Game 3 of the Winnipeg series, the Blues had gone 6 of 14 on the power play, or 42.9 percent. But the Stars have one of the league's top penalty kill units. They ranked fifth in the regular season (82.8 percent) and went through the entire first round of the playoffs without allowing a power-play goal.

The Blues got them once in Game 1 on a Vladimir Tarasenko goal but couldn't get much going Saturday with the man (and two-man) advantage.

"They did a good job up ice on us and disrupted our breakout at times," Berube said. "Winning the faceoff is

Stars goalie Ben Bishop turns to see the puck in the net after getting hit by Jaden Schwartz, who re-directed the puck into the goal while crashing into Bishop during the 4-2 loss to Dallas.

important, obviously. We lost some draws, and (that) kills your momentum a little bit. We had some good looks but not enough."

Speaking of faceoffs, the Blues won only three of 10 during those five power plays — losing each of the first seven such faceoffs.

Power play woes notwithstanding, Dallas took control of this game during even-strength play, albeit 4-on-4 play when Tarasenko and the Stars' Jamie Benn were both in the box for roughing 13 minutes into the game.

Three goals were scored over a 72-second stretch of 4-on-4, and two of them belonged to Dallas — stretching what had been a 1-0 Stars lead to 3-1. On both Dallas goals during this stretch, by rookie Miro Heiskanen and Mattias Janmark, the Blues were victimized by the Stars' transition game.

"We've got to make a better puck decision in the neutral zone, and then back our defense up on the play," Berube said. "A few mistakes on that."

A few mistakes in Round 2 of the Stanley Cup playoffs can send you into the offseason. But just like the Winnipeg series, the Blues expected a tough time with Dallas, and it looks like that's exactly what they're going to get.

"It's not going to be easy," said Binnington, who lost to the Stars for the third time this season. "These teams are here for a reason."

"It's gonna be what we expected, one-goal games," said Parayko, who scored the Blues' first goal and assisted on the Schwartz score. "They played well. And we're looking forward to going down there. ... We're a good road team. So it's gonna be good." ■

BLUES 4, STARS 3
APRIL 29, 2019 • DALLAS, TEXAS

ROAD WARRIORS

MAROON RESCUES BLUES WITH LATE GAME-WINNER

BY JIM THOMAS

It was wild. It was woolly. It was Pat Maroon with the game winner a mere 98 seconds before the end of regulation.

With two of the best defensive teams in the NHL on the ice at American Airlines Center, there were four goals scored in a stretch of 5 minutes 16 seconds down the stretch. The Blues scored last — Maroon's second goal of the playoffs — to claim a 4-3 victory.

Included in those hectic, frantic, unbelievable closing minutes the Blues allowed a shorthanded goal. And with just 43.3 seconds remaining they were guilty (for the second time Monday) of delay of game for shooting the puck over the glass.

There was a time when such a 1-2 punch of misfortune would've crushed the Blues. And there was a time Maroon couldn't buy a goal — with U.S. or Canadian currency. But the Blues are living in a different world these days.

"I think once we became the team that we became, went on a roll for quite some time, we were a confident group," interim coach Craig Berube said. "Just because a goal goes in, no matter if it's shorthanded or 5-on-5, we stay with it and keep battling.

"That's where we're at now. It's mental. I talked about mental toughness all year with this group — we're a mentally tough team now."

They're also a team that's 2-1 in this Western Conference semifinal series, with Game 4 coming up.

When a best-of-seven series is tied 1-1, the Game 3 winner ends up taking the series 67.4 percent of the time in NHL history.

Make of that what you will.

For now, the stat that matters is this: The Blues are 4-0 on the road this postseason, and all four have been one-goal games.

"I think we've won every (playoff) game by one goal," Alex Pietrangelo said. "See, I know that."

But 4-0 on the road in Winnipeg and now Dallas — how does that happen?

"That just means we're finding ways to win," Pietrangelo said. "It's not always pretty. It's not always the way we scripted it and drew it up before the game. It'd be nice to kind of get a lead and hold onto that. But this time of the year it can be unpredictable."

For sure.

After Andrew Cogliano's shorthanded goal with 6:54 to play tied it at 2-all, Pietrangelo beat Stars goalie Ben Bishop with what looked like a rising knuckle-puck to the near side to reclaim the lead just 17 seconds after the end of that ill-fated Blues power play.

"I wouldn't call it a howitzer," Pietrangelo said. "There wasn't much room there. I was just trying to get high-blocker and I got him dropping early. It's not going to go in like that every time. It did this time."

Dallas counter-punched 88 seconds later when Tyler Seguin beat Carl Gunnarsson in front of the net to tie it again — at 3-3.

But the Maroon-Tyler Bozak-Robert Thomas line was all over the ice Monday night. Cycling, hounding pucks and scoring goals.

"I wouldn't want to play against them, I tell you," Pietrangelo said. "They wear you down. They might not get one the first period, they might not get one the second period. But as the game goes on, they're gonna wear you down."

The line actually did get one in the second period when Bozak darted in for a tip-in of a Thomas shot for a 2-1 Blues

Jaden Schwartz celebrates after scoring the first goal in the 4-3 St. Louis win in Game 3.

lead. And then the Big Rig — Maroon — pulled up to the net.

He was wide open on the right side of the net when he flipped in the game-winner, high and far side. How does a guy that big (6-3, 225) find himself so open?

"He can kind of create space for himself," Vince Dunn said. "If you kind of miss a step on a guy that big, it's pretty hard to get back in his way. He's a big strong guy off (the puck) and with the puck."

Esa Lindell of the Stars was defending Maroon net front, but then all of a sudden Maroon was by himself.

"I think he just fell over me," Maroon said.

"We were just battling and he tried to get the edge on me and he fell on me."

Well, there might have been just a little (wink, wink) push by Maroon. But after Lindell was penalized for embellishment late in the second period — after not one but two flops that would have made a soccer player proud — Maroon would've had to drive a Big Rig over the Dallas defense for the play to be wiped out.

"I got an opportunity to use my hands in front and get the puck up quick," Maroon said. "At first, I didn't know if it went in. But we found a way to get it in and we found a way to win tonight."

But it didn't become a Gloria game —you know, that victory song — until the Blues killed off a delay of game penalty on Colton Parayko over the last 43.3 seconds.

"Parry takes the penalty," Pietrangelo said. "It's just bad ice and it rolls on him. That's how it is this time of year. So you find a way to win, you find a way to pick each other up and bail each other out. That's what we did."

So there continues to be no place like road for the Blues this postseason.

"I can't explain it," Berube said. ▨

Pat Maroon (7) starts to celebrate with teammate Colton Parayko (55) after Maroon scored what turned out to be the winning goal in a thrilling Game 3.

STARS 4, BLUES 2
MAY 1, 2019 • DALLAS, TEXAS

COOLED OFF

BLUES LOSE THEIR COOL AS DESPERATE STARS TIE PLAYOFF SERIES

BY JIM THOMAS

The Blues couldn't take the fifth Wednesday in Dallas, so now this Western Conference semifinal series moves to a fifth game tied 2-2 — just like their Round 1 series against Winnipeg.

In search of a franchise-record fifth consecutive playoff road victory, the Blues instead lost an early lead, lost their cool, and lost the game 4-2 before 18,790 at American Airlines Center.

After an early power play goal by Vladimir Tarasenko, things went downhill quickly for the Blues. Dallas scored the game's next four goals to take a 4-1 lead after two periods, with the Blues clearly frustrated as the Stars' lead mounted.

That was clear as day in the final minute of the second period.

First, David Perron took an ill-advised whack at the back of Ben Bishop with about a minute left in the period as the Stars goalie was attempting to clear the puck from behind the net.

"I was reaching, trying to prevent him from playing," Perron said. "I don't know, he's 6-6, so he's a big guy."

It looked like the textbook definition of a slash, but no penalty was called, probably because Bishop reacted as if stuck with a cattle prod. It must be a Stars thing. (See: Esa Lindell, flopping.)

And just as the period ended, Binnington and Stars forward Jamie Benn got into it in front of the St. Louis net. Binnington got two minutes for roughing; Benn got two minutes for unsportsmanlike conduct.

"There's nothing really to comment about," Benn said. "Just a bunch of grown men being donkeys out there."

Included in this case of "men being donkeys" was Benn slashing Binnington in a very, uh, sensitive area — an area below the belt.

"Good eye," Binnington said, answering a reporter's question on the target area of the slash.

Binnington responded with a shove or two, hence the roughing penalty. Previously a picture of composure with the Blues, Binnington then got an additional two minutes for slashing Bishop before the teams left the ice at the end of the period, thus giving the Stars a power play at the start of the third period.

When asked if he did something to Bishop, Binnington replied: "No. Just skating off. Emotions were high, I came back in here and regrouped. It's playoff hockey."

Bishop saw things differently, saying Binnington gave him a whack.

"I wasn't looking," Bishop said. "I didn't even know that he was there. He just hit my stick."

Interim coach Craig Berube said he didn't think his team lost its composure during this stretch.

There were plenty of dissenting views on that opinion.

"I thought they lost a bit of their emotional control," Stars coach Jim Montgomery said.

"Yeah, we've got to try and stay out of it," Perron said. "I think guys were just trying to get a spark maybe."

"I think we've got to be better for sure in that area," Ryan O'Reilly said. "It's something we talked about. I think we'll regroup here, we'll address that and move on."

Even so, the emotional fraying of the Blues didn't hurt them on the scoreboard.

The most telling sequence of the game actually occurred on a power play goal by Jason Spezza with just five seconds left on the penalty and only 51.8 seconds left in the first period.

"It's tough," Berube said. "I thought we did a good job killing that. The shot goes off 'Bo' (Jay Bouwmeester) and in. Yeah, it's tough, that's a tough one to give up for sure."

Binnington didn't leave much space, but also was screened with Bouwmeester right in front of him. Compounding matters was the fact that Tyler Bozak was in the box because of a dubious interference call — he stuck his rump out a bit in an apparent effort to impede a pursuing Dallas defender. Given the general mayhem of playoff hockey, does something like that merit blowing a whistle?

Berube said he was surprised at the Bozak call. "But again, things happen," he said. "I can't change it now."

Robert Bortuzzo and goalie Jordan Binnington react after the Stars scored their second goal in the 4-2 Game 4 loss.

Dallas didn't score in the third period, the Blues got a goal from rookie Robert Thomas — his first NHL playoff goal — with 6:16 to play against a stick-less Bishop. Less than two minutes later, O'Reilly came oh-so-close when he banged the puck off Bishop's pads from behind the goal and the puck bounced back towards the goal line.

Replays showed the puck might have crossed the goal line but were inconclusive. There was no stoppage of play for a review by the NHL situation room in Toronto.

The Blues outshot Dallas 12-5 in the third, but too little, too late. Dallas took the play to the Blues for most of two periods.

"They came out with more urgency than we did," said O'Reilly, who had two assists. "Obviously it's good to get the first goal, but we didn't respond well. They played better than us when you look at the whole game. We had some good things at times but our consistency wasn't there."

On Wednesday morning, the Stars talked about how they needed to compete harder against the Blues. They mentioned how they needed to limit the Blues' cycling and puck possession behind the net. They vowed to be stout defending their own net front.

Dallas checked all those boxes Wednesday night. And just checked the Blues in general.

"They were desperate, and we didn't match that desperation in the first two periods," Berube said. "We did in the third and we played a good period."

As the series shifts to Enterprise Center in St. Louis on Friday, the Stars have to feel good about where they stand. For them, this has a familiar feel to it. In their opening round against Nashville, they were down 2-1 in the series, blitzed the Predators 5-1 in Game 4 at American Airlines and proceeded to win the next two contests to take the series 4-2.

"Yeah, this is exactly where we are supposed to be at this point," said Jason Dickinson, who scored the first Dallas goal. "We are supposed to be 2-2. You know, it's now a three-game series, we've got to go take care of business there."

But the Blues pretty much feel the same way, because they're in the exact same spot as they were in Round 1. Only this time, they have home ice advantage if the series goes seven games.

"Yeah, it's a best-of-3 now," Binnington said. "We've been in this position before, so hopefully we handle it appropriately and just stick to our game." ∎

STARS 2, BLUES 1
MAY 3, 2019 • ST. LOUIS, MISSOURI

ON THE BRINK

BLUES' UNEXPECTED JOYRIDE ON THE VERGE OF ENDING WITH A THUD

BY JIM THOMAS

So it has come to this. The Blues are on the brink of elimination after Friday's 2-1 loss to the Dallas Stars. For the first time this postseason, they are down in a series — trailing three games to two.

A loss Sunday in Dallas ends this unexpected joyride with a thud.

"Got to win or you go home, simple as that," Jaden Schwartz said. "Desperation level needs to be the highest it's ever been. Got to play our best game and we feel confident going in there (to Dallas)."

The home bounce back the Blues desperately needed after Wednesday's 4-2 setback in Dallas never materialized. The Blues trailed 2-0 after two periods but couldn't quite recreate the Manitoba Miracle.

They also trailed 2-0 after two periods in that one — Game 5 of a Winnipeg series also tied two games apiece. They rallied on the road for a dramatic 3-2 victory, turning that series around.

Not so Friday, although they came close with Schwartz's third-period goal narrowing the Dallas lead to 2-1 and energizing a crowd of 18,542 that spent parts of the game booing the home team. Alas, there was no Escape at Enterprise for the Blues.

Dallas goalie Ben Bishop, the former Blue and Chaminade College Prep product, was excellent in stopping 38 of 39 Blues shots. That tied a Dallas postseason record for saves in a regulation game.

"Ben Bishop was the best player in the game tonight," Stars coach Jim Montgomery said. "I thought the Blues were the better team than we were tonight, but Ben Bishop was the difference. He's been the difference for us many times this year."

It was hard to argue that point, and Craig Berube didn't.

"He played a great game," Berube said. "Our goalie kept us in there, too, and played a good game. Made a lot of big saves. Both goalies played well. We have to find a way to get more goals."

Jordan Binnington did in fact keep the Blues in the game by stopping numerous Dallas breakaways.

"I think he stopped four breakaways and a couple 2-on-1s, so we could have extended the lead, but we couldn't," Montgomery said.

Sure enough, it could've easily been, say, 4-1 Dallas were it not for Binnington's breakaway magic.

Then again, even with all those saves by Bishop, he left a lot of rebounds out there for the taking. But for one reason or another the Blues couldn't get to many. They simply didn't have a whole lot going net front.

"We just have to get inside more," Schwartz said. "Pucks were laying there, we just have to find a way to get inside, get body position, and get a little more traffic."

"There were some pucks in between his legs that we just couldn't get to," Alex Pietrangelo said. "I think we can be a little bit more aggressive in front of him."

The Blues' power play was feeble most of the game. They were able to muster only five shots with the man advantage against the Stars' elite penalty kill unit. Not nearly good enough. For the series, the Stars have killed 14 of 16 Blues power plays — or 87.5 percent.

"Breakouts," Brayden Schenn said. "I don't think we're entering the zone as good as we can. It's making it pretty tough on each other. We're kind of putting each other in bad spots.

"I think execution has gotta be way better. As soon as the execution picks up, then the swagger will come, the confidence will come and that's when we start getting chances."

The Blues suddenly are running out of time to regain their swagger. They have now lost four of six this postseason at Enterprise Center. The home ice advantage they built up over the final three months of the regular season has vanished.

Trailing 2-0 entering the third period, Berube put his lines in a blender. He went with Schwartz-Schenn-Vladimir Tarasenko on one line. Robby Fabbri-Ryan O'Reilly-David Perron on another.

Jaden Schwartz is tripped in between Stars Miro Heiskanen and goalie Ben Bishop during the second period of Game 5. The Blues were tripped up as well, dropping the game and putting them one loss away from elimination.

The fourth line consisted of Oskar Sundqvist-Ivan Barbashev-Alexander Steen. That meant the only unchanged line was the third: Pat Maroon-Tyler Bozak-Robert Thomas.

Despite the switches, the Blues looked tentative, maybe even a little tight, in the early minutes of the period. But then Pietrangelo sent a harmless looking long-distance shot in on Bishop. Bishop was getting crowded by an onrushing Thomas and muffed his clearing attempt.

The puck found its way to Schwartz who beat Bishop near side at the 8:26 mark to make it a 2-1 game. A crowd that was booing just seconds earlier erupted in delight. Before you knew it, instead of boos it was "Let's go Blues!" in Enterprise.

It was Schwartz's seventh goal of the postseason. During the regular season, he didn't score his seventh goal until March 12. The Blues kept the pressure going after that, drawing a penalty on Jamie Benn for hooking Schenn with 11:13 to play.

The Blues got nothing done on that power play, but with just 4:14 to play Sundqvist had an excellent chance to tie the game, maneuvering in front of the Dallas net and getting Bishop down on the ice. Bishop was beat, but Sundqvist couldn't lift his shot over the goalie's pads.

"I saw him there," Bishop said. "And then he started to go around me. Just desperation. Throw your leg out there and luckily he hit it."

That was the Blues' last best chance. They pulled Binnington with a minute left, and finished out the game buzzing around Bishop, but couldn't finish. As a result, they're almost finished for the 2018-19 season.

"We played a pretty solid game I'd have to say," Schenn said. "I think guys were physical, blocking shots, doing what it takes to try and win any way (possible). Playoffs are tough. It's a game of mistakes. We didn't really make big mistakes on their goals but I guess big enough for them to end up in the back of the net."

Just 2:42 into the game Jason Spezza, left alone in front, sent a roof shot past Binnington after a pass from Tyler Seguin behind the net. The goal came right after Binnington turned away Mattias Janmark on a 2-on-1 break just seconds earlier.

Esa Lindell's first career playoff goal at the 6:13 mark of the second, made it 2-0. Once again, the Blues had problems with the Dallas transition game, with the Blues backing in, and then Lindell's backhand bouncing off the foot of Jay Bouwmeester and deflecting past Binnington. ∎

BLUES 4, STARS I
MAY 5, 2019 • DALLAS, TEXAS

BACK IN BUSINESS

PERRON AND BLUES REGROUP AFTER FRIDAY FLOP, BRING THE SERIES BACK TO ST. LOUIS

BY JIM THOMAS

David Perron had no idea. He didn't see his game-winning shot go past Dallas goalie Ben Bishop. In fact, he didn't see the puck coming to his stick on a pinpoint pass from Oskar Sundqvist. Really.

"I honestly never saw the puck," Perron said. "I didn't even see it go in. The guys just grabbed me and I was excited."

Perron's first goal of this series came late in the second period. The real excitement didn't come until later, after the final horn sounded to give the Blues a 4-1 victory in Game 6 of this Western Conference semifinal series.

St. Louis, are you ready for Game 7 Tuesday at Enterprise Center?

Ready or not, here it comes. Let's face it, after Dallas took control of this series with a 2-1 victory Friday in St. Louis, things looked bleak for the Blues. But in his pregame media session Sunday before a handful of reporters, interim coach Craig Berube was calm and confident as could be.

"We all believe we're going back for Game 7," Berube said 1½ hours before puck drop. "Why wouldn't we?"

Berube believes in his team; his team believes in him. Call it a mutual belief forged through months of hockey. Through disappointment, desperation and triumph. That feeling of belief permeated the visitors' locker room before Game 6, and even well before that.

"We felt like that after Game 5, and we felt even more like that the next morning," Perron said. "It's always hard for everyone. Mostly the way we played at certain times in the last game, where the crowd kind of gets on us — things like that.

"It's tough on us when that happens for sure. So we had to regroup and we did, and we're going to have to do that again and even play better next game."

After Perron's goal snapped a 1-1 tie at American Airlines Center, the Blues added goals by Jaden Schwartz and Sammy Blais — yes, Sammy Blais — in the third period. This marked the first time in the postseason that the Blues have won by more than one goal.

But it's not the first time this season the Blues outplayed a team in the final period. Through the Winnipeg and Dallas series the goal tally is Blues 11, Opponents 2 on the road in the third period.

There was some controversy involved with Schwartz's goal because of an injury to Bishop. The former Blue and Chaminade College Prep product took a blast from Colton Parayko — he of the 100 mph slapshot — off his shoulder/collarbone area.

Bishop fell to the ice in pain but there was no stoppage in play. Alexander Steen pounced on the loose puck and passed it to Schwartz, who deflected it in with 12 minutes 23 seconds left to play. It was Schwartz's eighth goal of this postseason; he didn't score his eighth goal of the regular season until March 19.

Some Stars felt play should have stopped while Bishop was down and shaken up, but there wasn't a ton of complaints on the subject from the Dallas side. All told, just four seconds elapsed between Parayko's shot and Schwartz's goal.

"It's the referee's discretionary call," Stars coach Jim Montgomery said. "We gotta keep playing, we gotta keep fighting through that. You can't be a ref. They're doing a good job and they're at this level of the Stanley Cup playoffs for a reason, and they thought there was no reason to blow the whistle. Our players have to play through stuff."

So the goal stood. The Blues had a 3-1 lead, a lead that expanded to 4-1 just 33 seconds later when Blais beat Bishop on a breakaway after a quick feed from Ryan O'Reilly. The Stars

Carl Gunnarsson and David Perron congratulate Sammy Blais after he scored the fourth goal in the 4-1 Blues win. The Game 6 victory forced a decisive Game 7 in St. Louis.

were done for Game 6, and so was Bishop. He was replaced by backup Anton Khudobin following the Blais goal.

In a bold move by Berube, Blais was inserted into the lineup for the first time since March 12 and played on the second line with Perron and Ryan O'Reilly. He replaced Robby Fabbri.

How bold of a move was it for Berube?

"He's got some (guts)," Perron said.

Despite the third-period proceedings, the goal that tilted the game — and perhaps the series — was Perron's. At that stage of the game, tied 1-1, Dallas was on the verge of taking control, piling up offensive zone time and making it hard for the Blues to get anything going.

You had the sense the next goal would be huge, and it was.

Ivan Barbashev chipped the puck down the right boards, Sundqvist carried it deep and passed net front to Perron.

"I looked at taking the shot and I had a pretty bad angle," Sundqvist said. "I saw Perron on the backdoor and I know he's got a heavy stick, and he's good at (being) in that area. I'm happy that he got that puck in. It's nice to see."

Except that Perron, well, he didn't see anything.

"I don't think I've ever scored a goal like that where I kind of — not guess, you know when it's coming," Perron said. "But you just kind of get the momentum into it and see what happens basically. And it worked out."

It worked out well enough to get the Blues back to St. Louis for Game 7. It will be the seventh time they will play a seventh game at home. They are 4-2 in the previous Game 7s, most recently a 3-2 win over Chicago in Round 1 of the 2016 playoffs.

"We're just excited to keep playing hockey," Perron said.

He was so excited for Game 6, he woke up at 4 a.m. Sunday before calming himself down and getting back to sleep.

"That's what it's all about, obviously," Perron continued. "We want to get to the end. But we're excited to keep it alive and do the same thing again next game." ▪

David Perron (middle) celebrates with Ivan Barbashev (left) and Joel Edmundson (right) after he scores in the second period of the critical road win.

BLUES 2, STARS I (2OT)
MAY 7, 2019 • ST. LOUIS, MISSOURI

SURVIVE AND ADVANCE

HOMETOWN HERO MAROON DELIVERS BLUES TO HOCKEY'S FINAL FOUR WITH GAME 7 WINNER

BY JIM THOMAS

On Monday, Pat Maroon told reporters Game 7 against the Dallas Stars would come down to "who wanted it more."

So how bad did Maroon want it? Especially when he saw that puck laying on the ice — in front of the Dallas net — less than six minutes into the second overtime Tuesday at Enterprise Center?

"I wanted it," Maroon said grinning like, well, someone who just scored a dramatic game-winning, Game 7 goal in double overtime. "That's the biggest goal I ever scored.

"I wanted it. If I missed that, I'd be getting a lot of boos maybe."

He didn't miss. His shot went in. The Blues were 2-1 winners over the Dallas Stars, winning the Western Conference semifinal series 4-3. Instead of boos, there was delirium among the 18,531 at Enterprise Center. Never has "Gloria" sounded so glorious.

"We found a way," captain Alex Pietrangelo said.

Since the beginning of the calendar year, when they were dead last in the National Hockey League, they've almost always found a way. Why is that?

"I couldn't tell you," goalie Jordan Binnington said. "We've got a strong group in here and we believe in ourselves. We're disciplined and composed. It's just been working for us."

"These guys in here never give up," Maroon said. "You can feel it in us. You can see it in guys' eyes. Every shift. The determination."

At no point was that more clear than when Robert Thomas' shot hit the post, bounced off the back of the head of Dallas goalie Ben Bishop and plopped to the ice. The hockey gods were smiling on the Blues, and Maroon was there to take advantage.

"As a team, we knew eventually they were gonna crack," said Thomas, the 19-year old rookie who blossomed in this series.

Perhaps. But surely Thomas didn't think it would take

54 shots on goal for Bishop to crack. Thomas giggled — yes, giggled — at the thought.

"No, I don't think so," Thomas said. "If you asked me before the game if it was gonna take (54) shots to finally break it for a second goal, I wouldn't believe you. That was pretty crazy and a great performance by (Bishop)."

Dinged in the collarbone by a Colton Parayko shot on Sunday in Game 6, Bishop was spectacular Tuesday. His 52 saves were a career high. In three Game 7's during Bishop's NHL career, he has stopped 105 of 107 shots.

The only ones he missed came Tuesday night — Vince Dunn's first career playoff goal at the 13:30 mark of the first period. And Maroon's game-winner.

It was the second time this series that Oakville beat Chaminade. Maroon, who attended Oakville High, also beat Bishop — a Chaminade College Prep product — for the game-winner with 1:38 to play in Game 3, a 4-3 Blues win.

They know each other, they played golf together last summer. And now Maroon has bragging rights.

But the real moment for Maroon came when he saw his son Anthony after Tuesday's game-winner, crying in the stands. Tears of joy.

"I saw him and I pointed to him," Maroon said. "I'm proud. I'm proud to be from St. Louis and I'm proud to put that jersey on every night. And I'm proud to work hard in front of these fans.

"And to work hard for these (teammates) that deserve it in here, that have been here for so long and want nothing more than to win. Right now, that's Round 2 and we've got to go onto Round 3."

Yes, for the second time in four years, but just the fourth time in the last 33 years, the Blues are in the conference final. They are in hockey's Final Four, just four wins removed from the Stanley Cup Final.

They meet the winner of Wednesday's game between the

St. Louis Blues fans cheer as Pat Maroon is mobbed by teammates after scoring the winning goal in double overtime to beat the Dallas Stars in Game 7 and advance to the Western Conference Final.

San Jose Sharks and Stan Kroenke's Colorado Avalanche.

"It's a grind," interim coach Craig Berube said. "That's why it's a grind of the Stanley Cup playoffs. It's a lot of work, but it's very rewarding. We're moving on to the third round and we're excited. Guys are ready to roll."

Binnington wasn't as busy as Bishop, but he stopped 29 of 30 shots including some huge saves in overtime. After getting the best of 2018 Vezina Trophy finalist Connor Hellebuyck of Winnipeg in Round 1, he helped the Blues get past 2019 Vezina finalist Bishop in Round 2.

"I was pretty tired out there," Binnington said. "I was pretty happy to see that (Maroon) puck go in, and in front of a home crowd, the atmosphere was crazy. It was a fun experience."

Binnington stopped Jamie Benn on a wraparound in the second overtime, just 1½ minutes before Maroon's game-winner. With about six minutes left in the first overtime, Andrew Cogliano had Binnington down and looked to have him beat. But Binnington stuck a leg out, and the puck bounced wide.

"I just got the pad out there," Binnington said. "I'm not really thinking at that point, I'm just trying to focus as hard as I can and hope for the best."

Moments earlier, Andrew Radulov charged hard to the net and crashed into Binnington, taking his legs out from under him. The crowd booed, Binnington needed a couple of minutes to gather himself, but was OK.

"Those skinny legs held up there," Binnington said. "Right?"

Among star St. Louis athletes, Binnington has the skinniest legs this side of Isaac Bruce. Right?

"Watch it!" Binnington joked.

In contrast, there's nothing skinny about Maroon. The player known as the "Big Rig" appeared to deflect Dunn's shot past Bishop 13½ minutes into the game for the game's first score. But the goal was credited to Dunn, the first goal allowed by Bishop in three Game 7's as an NHL player.

The Blues and their fans enjoyed that 1-0 lead for only 2½ minutes. During a strange sequence in which the Blues had trouble clearing the zone, David Perron attempted to bank the puck off the end boards behind the net.

Not only did the puck hit referee Marc Joannette in the skate, Joannette then kicked the puck off the post and in front of the net, right to Mats Zuccarello who scored into a largely open net.

"It was just a series of unfortunate events," Binnington said. "I kinda lost sight of the puck because I thought it was going behind the net. I saw Big Ed (Joel Edmundson) trip on my stick so it was a disaster. Then they just got the goal. All you can do is just pick up your stuff and get back at it."

More than three hours later, the Blues were able to pack up their stuff — for the night. Round 3 awaits. ∎

Pat Maroon was already a hometown hero before his unforgettable goal and now will go down in St. Louis sports lore.

SHARKS 6, BLUES 3
MAY 11, 2019 • SAN JOSE, CALIFORNIA

THE FIRST TEST

MISTAKE-PRONE BLUES GIVE AWAY GAME 1 TO SHARKS

BY JIM THOMAS

The foundation of the Blues team — its defense — knew it would be tested against the high-scoring San Jose Sharks in this Western Conference final. They get at least three more chances, but on Saturday at SAP Center, they failed the first test.

Logan Couture opened and closed the scoring with goals, Timo Meier scored two goals to close out the second period, and when all was said and done the Sharks put a six-pack of goals in the back of the net, taking Game 1 of the series 6-3.

The six goals matched the most given up by the Blues this postseason — they lost 6-3 to Winnipeg in Game 3 of that first-round series. And they have lost a series opener for the first time in these playoffs.

"There were a few too many mistakes out there, (and) whenever there was, they capitalized on the chances they got," Joel Edmundson said. "I think that was the biggest difference of tonight's game."

The Sharks averaged 3.52 goals per game in the regular season, second best in the NHL. So they don't really need any help to find the net. But they got plenty from the Blues, in the form of costly giveaways. Their neutral zone play was a nightmare.

"We got really outplayed in the neutral zone," Ryan O'Reilly said. "We didn't take care of the puck well enough. ... A lot of speed coming at us. And we just didn't manage it. We just didn't manage it the right way.

"We might have been trying to feel it out a little bit too much. But we know we have to be better and work harder for each other. That wasn't our best tonight."

The Sharks' sixth goal came into an empty net, but at least three of the first five were fueled by miscues in the neutral zone.

OK, maybe the first of those three wasn't really a miscue. In fact, maybe it should've been a cross-checking penalty against Meier. In any event, San Jose took a 1-0 lead when Meier knocked down Alex Pietrangelo from behind, creating an instant 2-on-1 break for the Sharks. Couture finished it off

for his league-high 10th postseason goal. (It would be 11 goals after his empty-netter.)

Jordan Binnington had no chance on the play.

"I thought we were hard on pucks in certain areas, (and) on our forecheck we were good," Couture said. "We were able to outmuscle them. On my goal, Timo did a great job at the blueline, knocking Pietrangelo down and then we got our second man there."

Pietrangelo saw it a little differently, saying: "He's not even going for the puck."

Kevin Labanc, who scored the game-winner in overtime when the Blues last played here on March 16, gave the Sharks a 3-1 lead on a play when Edmundson's chip into the neutral zone landed right on the stick of a San Jose player, starting a rush the other way.

Another giveaway in the neutral zone, this time by Colton Parayko, made it 4-2 San Jose. Couture poked the puck loose near the St. Louis blue line and Meier swooped in, raced past Jay Bouwmeester around the edge and sent a backhand past Binnington.

"The first two periods we didn't find our game," Robert Thomas said. "We didn't really get it in deep. We were turning it over and feeding their transition. You know, they play fast and through the neutral zone. They transition really quick. So I think it was just mistakes on our part,"

But it wasn't a turnover or misplay that gave the Sharks the lead for good. A couple of costly penalties gave San Jose a 5-on-3 power play in the first period, which the Sharks turned into a goal.

The Blues went the entire Game 7 double-overtime victory Tuesday against Dallas without a penalty assessed against them. In fact, when Bouwmeester was sent off for interference at the 9:36 mark of the first period, the Blues had set an all-time NHL playoff record for going the longest time without a penalty — 136 minutes 20 seconds of ice time.

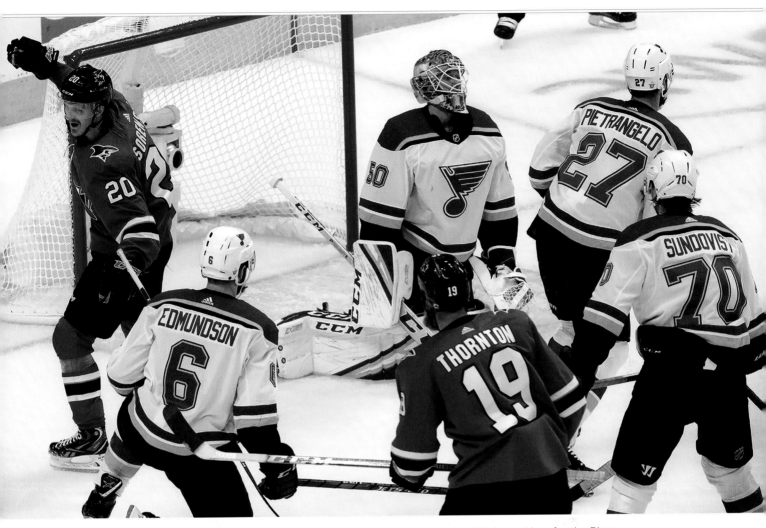

San Jose's Marcus Sorensen (left) celebrates after the Sharks score during the 6-3 Game 1 loss for the Blues.

Just 57 seconds after Bouwmeester was sent off his partner on the Blues' second defensive pairing — Parayko — joined him after slashing Evander Kane.

That gave the Sharks a 5-on-3 advantage for the next 63 seconds. It was the first 5-on-3 the Blues had to defend in the postseason after facing six 5-on-3 penalty kills in the regular season.

(The last being Feb. 12 against the New Jersey Devils.)

Coach Craig Berube couldn't really complain about those calls.

"They're penalties," Berube said. "Tough one on Bouwmeester a little bit, but a lot of that goes on both ways. We got called for it and Parayko breaks a guy's stick. He's going to call that to make it a 5-on-3."

The Sharks had just nine seconds left on the 5-on-3 when Binnington made an impressive pad save on Joe Pavelski.

While the puck was still in the air from the initial save, Pavelski batted the puck into the net to give San Jose a 2-1 lead at the 11:24 mark.

The Blues, who got goals by Edmundson, O'Reilly and Tyler Bozak, were fighting uphill on the scoreboard the rest of the game.

The Sharks were the quicker team, and they used it to their advantage. The up-and-down pace was a tempo more suited to the San Jose style of play. The absolute last thing the Blues wanted in this game — or this series — is a shootout with the Sharks. And that's what they got.

"They got a ton of great forwards out there that make a lot of plays," Thomas said. "We turned it over and we didn't get it in deep and make them work for it. When you give teams like that so many chances off the rush and you're not active in the zone, then they'll be able to make plays with it." ∎

BLUES 4, SHARKS 2
MAY 13, 2019 • SAN JOSE, CALIFORNIA

'WE'RE NOT GOING AWAY'

BLUES STORM BACK WITH IMPROBABLE WIN IN THE SHARK TANK

BY JIM THOMAS

A beaming Tom Stillman, in the hallway outside the Blues' locker room, couldn't help himself.

"I had Bortuzzo, backhand, top shelf, from the slot," Stillman deadpanned, minutes after yet another improbable Blues victory.

OK, the team's chairman and governor didn't actually make that prediction. Who could have seen that coming?

And he certainly wasn't the only one excited by Robert Bortuzzo's goal late in the second period, which turned out to be the game-winner.

After the Blues' 4-2 victory over San Jose at SAP Center, teammate Jaden Schwartz was asked if Bortuzzo ever made shots like that in practice? (Because he sure doesn't score many in games.)

Schwartz didn't hesitate: "All the time," he quipped.

While Bortuzzo sat center stage at the podium postgame — the rarest of seats for him — a reporter familiar with his background asked if Bortuzzo could remember his last playoff goal. He even offered a couple of hints... 2007... Kitchener Rangers.

Ring a bell?

Bortuzzo thought about it for a moment then conceded: "I don't."

He'll remember this one. In a thrill ride of a game, the Blues took a 2-0 lead, blew it in an instant, and seemingly were on the verge of cracking. All this after being humbled in a 6-3 Game 1 loss on Saturday.

Falling behind in the series 2-0 was a recipe for disaster. In franchise history, the Blues are 1-17 in the playoffs when losing the first two games of a series.

But Bortuzzo's goal — backhand, top-shelf, from the slot — broke the 2-2 tie with 3:26 left in the second and saved the Blues from facing that tough math.

Blues coach Craig Berube will remember it, too.

"That was a helluva backhand," he said, chuckling. "'Borts,' he finds a way to get open in the offensive zone. He does some real good things in there, jumping in at the right time. He doesn't obviously have the touch to produce all the time, but he scored a big one tonight for us."

This Western Conference finals series now is tied a game each, and despite that Game 1 loss Saturday, the Blues have taken over home-ice advantage.

The next two games are in St. Louis, starting Wednesday. And if this series goes the full seven games, three of the remaining five will be played at the House of Blues.

The Blues went 0 for 5 on the power play, allowed a shorthanded goal on one of them after an Alex Pietrangelo turnover, and before you could say "Logan Couture," their 2-0 lead become a 2-2 tie in just 1 minute 59 seconds.

The Shark Tank was about to come unhinged after those Couture goals — he has an NHL-high 13 for the playoffs. Even though the score was tied it felt like the Blues were trailing 4-1 judging by the crowd noise, the momentum, and all those Sharks circling around rookie goalie Jordan Binnington.

No need to even ask if Binnington was nervous, because you know the answer.

"You appreciate the thunder, right?" Binnington said. "This is the best part of sports, this time of year. It's why you play. You want to be that difference-maker. Obviously you don't want to let a goal in, but you notice that. You just keep moving forward."

Binnington is 9-2 in the games following losses in his rookie season. It's 10-2 (with a save percentage of .934) if you include an overtime loss to the New York Islanders in the regular season.

So just when you think the Blues are in severe trouble, they (almost) always find a way to get it done.

As forward Brayden Schenn put it, "We're not going

Oskar Sundqvist (foreground) celebrates with teammate Ivan Barbashev after Sundqvist scored the final goal of the Blues' 4-2 victory in Game 2.

away. It's playoff hockey. It's gonna be ups and downs, momentum shifts."

"We got four goals from four different players," defenseman Joel Edmundson said. "That's how we roll."

It sure is. Four goals and a victory, with none of the goal-scorers named Tarasenko, O'Reilly, Perron or Schenn.

"That's how we're built," Schenn said. "It's kinda been like that all year, whether the back end's scoring or guys are stepping up. We didn't have too many 20-goal scorers and we had 99 points on the season."

And here they are three victories away from a berth in the Stanley Cup finals.

On Monday, the goal-scorers were Jaden Schwartz (his ninth of the playoffs), Vince Dunn, Bortuzzo and Oskar Sundqvist.

It was the first postseason goal of Bortuzzo's NHL career. He had only two regular-season goals this season, and in 335 career regular-season games he has only 14 goals.

Throw in his 30 postseason games, and it was 14 goals in 365 total games — before Monday.

Although Bortuzzo couldn't remember that playoff goal with the Kitchener Rangers in 2007, San Jose coach Peter DeBoer probably can. He was the Kitchener coach that season in the Ontario Hockey League.

This was a night where Berube shuffled his defensive pairings and shuffled his power play units in an effort to settle things down after the Couture goals, both of which beat Binnington 5-hole.

The Blues are now 0 for 18 on the power play since a Vladimir Tarasenko goal in Game 4 of the Dallas series. Since the start of that Round 2 series against the Stars, the Blues are a paltry two for 28.

None of that mattered, however, when it got Sunny in San Jose late in the third period. On a nifty feed from Alexander Steen, Sundqvist scored his third postseason goal to make it a 4-2 game with just 3:08 to play.

"The only option is to put a backhand in, and it was nice to see the puck go in," Sundqvist said. "All the credit to 'Steener' for that pass."

That sent some of those rowdy San Jose fans to the exits, and the Blues back to St. Louis with renewed life.

"I didn't notice (fans leaving)," Sundqvist said. "You don't look up to the stands. I'm just trying to focus on the game. I don't need any more distractions.

"But obviously if that's what happened, it's always nice for a road team to be able to do that." ∎

Jordan Binnington makes a stop on a shot during the first period of Game 2. Binnington saved 24 of 26 shots in the game.

SHARKS 5, BLUES 4 (OT)
MAY 15, 2019 • ST. LOUIS, MISSOURI

A HELPING HAND

NHL DEALS CRUSHING LOSS TO BLUES

BY JIM THOMAS

In the 1985 World Series between St. Louis and Kansas City, there was the safe call by Don Denkinger.

In 1990 at Faurot Field, there was the "Fifth-Down" football game between Missouri and Colorado.

In 2002 in Super Bowl XXXVI between the St. Louis Rams and New England Patriots, there was "Spygate."

And now, on Wednesday at Enterprise Center in Game 3 of the Western Conference finals, the NHL brought us the "Hand-Pass" game.

With the score tied 4-4 in overtime, Timo Meier of the Sharks collided with Jay Bouwmeester of the Blues in the right faceoff circle. While on his knees, Meier batted the puck with his right hand to the front of the net and in the direction of San Jose defenseman Erik Karlsson.

But the puck didn't go very far. Gustav Nyquist got to the puck and passed to Karlsson, whose shot beat goalie Jordan Binnington at the 5-minute 23-second mark of overtime to give San Jose a controversial 5-4 victory.

By rule, Meier's hand pass was illegal and play should have been stopped because the puck was touched first by a teammate.

While the Sharks celebrated, Binnington and other Blues argued with the referees, who gathered near the scorer's table at center ice to discuss the situation. After maybe a minute or two, the goal stood and officials were escorted off the ice with debris showered on them from irate fans in the stands at Enterprise.

As he left the ice, Binnington banged his goalie stick hard against the ice in disgust. Brayden Schenn did the same.

So was it a hand pass, Craig Berube?

"What do you guys think?" Berube asked reporters.

"Yes," was the reply from more than one reporter.

"Then don't ask me. No reason to ask me," Berube replied.

When told that reporters wanted to hear what he had to say, Berube replied: "Nothing. I have nothing to say about it."

Berube said he got no explanation on the call. Or non-call.

It took the NHL more than 45 minutes after the game to offer an explanation via NHL series director Kay Whitmore.

"It's a non-reviewable play," Whitmore told a pool reporter.

When asked if any of the game officials saw the play, Whitmore replied: "What they told me? It's a non-reviewable play. You can read between the lines. You can figure out what you want. You watched the video. But it's just non-reviewable. I know that sounds like a cop-out answer, but that's the truth."

Meier was awarded an assist on the play, which is usually awarded — you know — after someone makes a pass.

So it's a crushing loss for the Blues, who rallied from a 2-0 deficit after one period with four goals in the second period to take a 4-3 lead. Only to have the Sharks send the game into overtime tied 4-4 on Logan Couture's net-front goal with 1:01 left in overtime.

San Jose now leads the series 2-1, with Game 4 set for Friday at Enterprise.

"Tough call, but nothing will change now," Blues general manager Doug Armstrong said via text after the game. "Need to prepare to play Friday."

Armstrong said he would have nothing else to say about the play. But he had plenty to say shortly after the game when he stormed by the officials' locker room, banged on the door and yelled, "(Bleeping) garbage!"

There were several Blues who commented on the play, although not as graphically, including captain Alex Pietrangelo.

"I guess they have a different set of rules for two different teams," Pietrangelo said. "I'm sure they will lose some sleep tonight after looking at it."

David Perron, who scored twice in a span of 2:39 in the second period to turn a 3-2 Blues deficit into a 4-3 Blues lead, was asked if it appeared to be a hand pass.

"Did it appear?" he replied sarcastically. "It was, but let's move forward and that's what we'll try to do here in the next 24 hours. We're a really good team in here.

"We feel our first 10 minutes were awesome and then they

The Blues' bench responds after the referees decided to allow the Sharks' winning goal despite a hand pass. The Blues dropped the game as a result, 5-4 in overtime.

score two goals, kind of put us on our heels, and we found a way to come back in the second with a good period. Then a really good third period. They get a bounce and we played well in overtime as well."

All well and good but how difficult is it to have a game end like that, in overtime, in the Stanley Cup playoffs?

"It's unacceptable, but it's OK," Perron said. "It's 2-1 right now."

The game would've never gone to overtime had the Blues been able to close out the game in regulation. Jaden Schwartz barely missed an empty-net goal near center ice that would have made it a 5-3 Blues lead with 1:44 left to play.

The Blues haven't made an empty-net goal since March 21 of the regular season against Detroit, with Ivan Barbashev scoring — his third goal of that night.

The Blues also had two icing plays by Pietrangelo that stopped the clock, resulted in faceoffs deep in the St. Louis zone, and allowed the Sharks to catch their breath.

"The first icing, that's a tough play, coming around the net," Berube said. "There really weren't a whole lot of options. He was trying to get it out of the zone. Obviously too hard.

"The second one though, on the draw, I think we can skate a little bit on that play and probably get the puck out without icing it. But listen, things happen, they're quick out there and not a lot of time. Things happen so you've just got to be better there.

"We've got to close that game out in my opinion. We should have won it 4-3."

But they didn't. In a game that could prove costly for the Blues in this series and have repercussions for years to come. ◼

BLUES 2, SHARKS 1
MAY 17, 2019 • ST. LOUIS, MISSOURI

FAIR AND SQUARE

BLUES SURVIVE FRANTIC FINISH AND TIE THE SERIES

BY JIM THOMAS

There was sheer madness in the closing minutes Friday at Enterprise Center. Nothing like the madness that engulfed Game 3 on Wednesday — the Hand Pass game. But madness, nonetheless.

Just ask rookie goalie Jordan Binnington, who stood strong in the frantic final 2 minutes 2 seconds of play with San Jose counterpart Martin Jones on the bench, the Sharks' net empty, and six attackers on the ice for the visiting team.

"I'm just trying to stay strong and obviously close it out," Binnington said. "After last game, especially. The team did a great job in front of me, battling hard, competing, staying disciplined. Faceoffs were huge, and boys were blocking shots everywhere.

"It's just madness, and you hope for the best and try to close the door."

Unlike Wednesday, when the Blues yielded a goal with 61 seconds left in regulation in what became a crushing 5-4 overtime loss, Binnington and the Blues conquered the madness.

Getting first-period goals from Ivan Barbashev and Tyler Bozak, the Blues held off the San Jose "Don't Call Us Lucky" Sharks, 2-1 in Game 4 of the Western Conference final.

Each of the Blues' three series have taken on a life of their own. But once again, for the third series in a row, they find themselves tied at 2-2. Game 5 is Sunday at the SAP Center.

Now just two victories removed from their first Stanley Cup finals appearance since 1970, the Blues feel if they play their game they can win this series.

"Oh definitely," coach Craig Berube said. "It's a close series for sure. They're a really good hockey team. You gotta play really well against them."

Berube liked the Blues' first period. Barbashev scored his first NHL playoff goal just 35 seconds in as the Blues came out flying. They had five prime scoring chances in the opening five

minutes but only one goal to show for it.

But if there were any doubts about a "Hand Pass" hangover from Game 3, when a blown call on an illegal hand pass by Timo Meier led to the game-winning goal by the Sharks, the Blues dispelled that early.

"It starts with our head coach," Brayden Schenn said. "'Chief' (Berube) came in, said don't worry about it, move on. Come to the rink the next day with a smile on your face, and guys did that. You can look at it two ways: You can come here and mope around and say, 'We got screwed,' or you can turn the page and move on, and I think that's what we did."

They turned the page, and they made it 2-0 late in the first period when Bozak scored a power-play goal with Meier sent off for hooking Ryan O'Reilly.

Vladimir Tarasenko rifled a wrist shot that Jones stopped but couldn't control. The puck was loose in front of the net, where Pat Maroon and Bozak whacked away furiously until there it was — the puck was in the back of the net and the goal light on.

It was Bozak's fourth goal of the postseason and his second postseason game-winner. And after an 0-for-18 power-play slump it made two power-play goals in two games for a reconfigured power-play unit.

"A good faceoff win by 'O'Ry,'" Bozak said. "We were stressing we had to get more pucks on net with traffic, and we kind of passed it around the outside a little too much. Great shot by Vladi. Patty made a tip, a loose puck in front. I'm kind of lucky it ended up on my stick and went in."

But after that strong first period, San Jose gradually took command of play, much to the chagrin of Berube.

"We gotta do a better job of not allowing them to take control of the game that way," he said. "I thought in the second period we just sat back too much. We didn't play aggressive enough in the second period."

Jordan Binnington blocks a shot while defenseman Colton Parayko defends against San Jose Sharks center Tomas Hertl during the second period of Game 4.

A period of 4-on-4 play midway through the second looked more like a San Jose power play. And for about 3½ minutes late in the second period, the Blues just couldn't get the puck out of their own zone.

The official game stats showed defenseman Jay Bouwmeester was on the ice for a whopping 3:47 during that stretch. The oldest Blues player at age 35, Bouwmeester undoubtedly slept well Friday night.

Things didn't change much for the Blues in the third period. San Jose kept pressuring, the Blues sat back, and then Tomas Hertl cut the lead in half with his first goal — and his first point — of the series. It was undoubtedly a goal Binnington would like to have back, with Brent Burns' shot trickling through his legs and Hertl getting behind Binnington to tap it in.

Otherwise, Binnington was strong all night, especially when the madness hit.

"As soon as people start doubting him, he pulls another sick performance," David Perron said. "We maybe relied on him a little too much the last two periods. That's something we can look at, but right now we're happy with the win and the result."

Well, Binnington did allow a total of 12 goals in Games 1-3 of the series, causing some observers to wonder if he was tiring with the strain of three series' worth of intense playoff hockey. He didn't look tired Friday, stopping 29 of 30 shots to register his 10th win of this postseason.

That set a Blues playoff record, held previously at nine games by Brian Elliott (2016) and Roman Turek (2001) — and by Binnington before Friday.

"That's a great honor, obviously," Binnington said. "I'm having a lot of fun back here playing with this team and they're doing a great job. They limited chances tonight. I think we played a complete game, so I just try do to my job."

San Jose had 73 total shot attempts to 35 for the Blues. But the Blues blocked 21 of those Sharks shots, their third-highest total of this postseason. And Binnington gets at least two more chances to pad that record win total.

And maybe more. ◼

St. Louis Blues center Ivan Barbashev (second from right) celebrates with teammates after scoring the first goal of the Blues' 2-1 win.

BLUES 5, SHARKS 0
MAY 19, 2019 • SAN JOSE, CALIFORNIA

TIPPING THE SCALES

BLUES SMELLING BLOOD AFTER DOMINATING SHARKS

BY JIM THOMAS

Hey, St. Louis. Lord Stanley is winking at you. He's got this fabulous Cup made of silver (and nickel alloy) that goes to the best team in the NHL. He just wants you to know that your hockey team is one victory away from being a finalist for the thing.

One victory. That's all it takes to send the Blues to the Stanley Cup finals for the first time since 1970 — nearly a half-century ago.

They're in this position because in Game 100 of the season — regular-season and postseason contests included — they absolutely pulverized the San Jose Sharks. It was 5-0 Blues on Sunday in Game 5 of the Western Conference final. They now lead the best-of-seven series 3-2.

After all this time, all the trials and tribulations, what would it mean for the Blues to get to the finals? St. Louis native Pat Maroon smiled broadly at the question. His eyes twinkled in delight, like a kid on Christmas morning. He gathered himself. Collected his thoughts.

"I don't want to comment on that, because I don't know what to say," Maroon said, chuckling for just a second. "But yeah, we're close. We're very close right now."

The Blues haven't clinched a Stanley Cup berth at home since Year 1 — the 1967-68 season — when Ron Schock's double-overtime goal gave them a 2-1 triumph over the Minnesota North Stars. They'll get a chance to do it again Tuesday at Enterprise Center, with puck drop shortly after 7 p.m.

Vladimir Tarasenko, who had a goal and three assists in the game Sunday, beamed at the thought of the finals.

"We've been playing for this one forever," he said. "I think every player dreams of playing in Stanley Cup final. But we're not there yet."

Even the normally stoic Jaden Schwartz, who had a hat trick — yes, another hat trick — grinned as well.

"You don't want to look too far ahead," Schwartz said. "We all know how important and how hard that last win's going to be. But yeah, it'd be a dream-come-true. That's really all I can say."

The Blues were simply superb Sunday. Better than the Game 6 clincher against Winnipeg in Round 1. Better than the Game 7 double-overtime clincher in Round 2 against Dallas, when they put 54 shots on goal and only Ben Bishop kept the Stars in the contest.

On Sunday, the Blues got the aforementioned hat trick from Schwartz, his third "hatty" in two months and his second of the postseason. He's the first player in Blues history with two hat tricks in a single postseason and the first NHL player to do so since Detroit's Johan Franzen did so in 2008.

Schwartz now has more goals in 18 playoff games (12) than he did in 69 regular-season games (11).

A single, solitary Blues hat was tossed to the ice in celebration at SAP Center when Schwartz got his third goal of the afternoon, with 3:58 to play. Word made it back to San Jose that many, many more hats were thrown to the ice at Enterprise Center, where thousands saw it happen on the giant video board at a Blues watch party.

"I heard it was wild at Enterprise Center today," Blues defenseman Joel Edmundson said. "We're looking forward to getting on home ice and hopefully we can close it out."

Tarasenko stretched his career-long postseason scoring streak to five games (two goals, five assists), with a key second-period goal on a penalty shot. It gave the Blues a 3-0 lead and was the first successful penalty shot in Blues postseason history.

"It was a great shot, obviously," coach Craig Berube said.

Tarasenko beat San Jose goalie Martin Jones high on his glove side, a target area the Blues have exploited all series.

But it was Oskar Sundqvist, the greatest out-of-nowhere

Blues interim coach Craig Berube yells at the refs during the first period of the dominating 5-0 win by St. Louis.

story for the Blues this side of Jordan Binnington, who gets credit for the game-winner. In what might have been Sundqvist's hardest shot of the season, he ripped a one-timer past Jones less than six minutes into the game after an errant pass by Sharks defenseman Erik Karlsson went between the legs of teammate Brenden Dillon and caromed off the side boards to Sundqvist.

After getting outplayed during the last two periods in Game 4 on Friday in St. Louis, the Blues did a 180 Sunday. Over the final two periods, they outshot the Sharks 36-10 and outscored them 4-0.

How do you explain that?

"Maybe it's just a snowball effect," said Binnington, who posted the first shutout by a rookie goalie in Blues postseason history.

"We don't play well in the second period" of Game 4, Tarasenko said. "So we pay a lot of attention to keep our game, and raise our level to the game. Don't sleep and give them easy chances."

San Jose came out smoking in the early minutes, but it didn't last. Evander Kane hit a goalpost a mere 12 seconds into the game.

"That was nice to hear the post," Binnington said. "Sometimes you get the bounces. They went all for us" this time.

Unfortunately for the Sharks, that proved to be their "highlight" for the day.

The physical Blues continued to pound away on the Sharks every chance they could, and the cumulative effect of 182 Blues hits throughout the series seemed to catch up with San Jose.

The Sharks finished the game minus four players, and mainstays Karlsson and Tomas Hertl did not come out at all in the third period.

As the score mounted, the Sharks lost their cool. Micheal Haley was given a game misconduct at the 7:13 mark of the third period for giving Alex Pietrangelo the business right after a faceoff. Exactly 10 minutes later, Kane got a game misconduct after a sequence in which he was whistled for goaltender interference on Binnington and also for slashing Edmundson.

"They can run around," Edmundson said of the Sharks. "But I think the refs handled it pretty good."

But Edmundson sent no chirping San Jose's way, at least not once the game ended.

"I'm not going to poke the bear or anything," he said. "We're just happy with the way we played and we kept our cool." ∎

San Jose's Kevin Labanc can't hit the puck past the pads of Jordan Binnington during the third period of Game 5. Binnington was terrific, shutting out the Sharks on 21 shots.

BLUES 5, SHARKS I
MAY 21, 2019 • ST. LOUIS, MISSOURI

GLORIOUS!

BLUES GO MARCHING IN TO STANLEY CUP FINALS AFTER 49-YEAR ABSENCE

BY JIM THOMAS

Stick taps to Glenn Hall and the Plager brothers, Jimmy Roberts and Ron Schock. To Red Berenson and Noel Picard. Al Arbour, Terry Crisp, Jacques Plante — the whole crew from the infancy of St. Louis Blues hockey. They laid the foundation and electrified this town a half-century ago with Stanley Cup finals appearances in each of the team's first three years of existence. Fellas, you now have company.

For the first time since 1970, the Blues are returning to the Cup finals. This town of toasted ravioli-crunching, pork steak-munching, Bud-guzzling Blues fans is electrified once more.

The Blues — yes, the Blues — are playing for the Cup, winning the Western Conference finals four games to two with a 5-1 victory Tuesday over the San Jose Sharks at Enterprise Center.

"I don't understand yet," said Vladimir Tarasenko, whose power-play goal late in the first period counts as the game-winner. "It's obviously a pretty big deal for us to get what we get. The feeling is we're not done yet.

"Really proud of the team how far we go, but there's still one more opponent to beat. It feels unbelievable. I'm not going to lie."

The last time the Blues made the Cup finals in 1970, they faced Bobby Orr and the Boston Bruins. Nearly a half-century later, they're back in the Cup and playing ... Patrice Bergeron, Brad Marchand, Tuukka Rask and the Boston Bruins in the Cup finals.

Game 1 is Monday in Boston.

Dead last in the 31-team NHL on Jan. 2, the Blues need four victories against Boston to complete their improbable worst-to-first journey.

"I always thought this was possible when looking at this group," said Ryan O'Reilly, the team's unofficial regular-season MVP who had three assists Tuesday. "But having the struggles we had early in the year and then rallying to be here now, it's amazing that we actually have a chance to win a Stanley Cup now."

They do. The Blues have never won a Stanley Cup. In fact, they've never even won a Stanley Cup game, getting swept by the Montreal Canadiens in 1968 and '69, and the Bruins in 1970. But as the clock wound down at Enterprise, and the crowd kept chanting "We want the Cup! We want the Cup!" all things seemed possible.

"To go through what we went through this year is not easy," said Alex Pietrangelo, who with an assist Tuesday set a Blues record for most points by a defenseman in one postseason (13). "I'm sure people questioned me (as captain) and questioned the group.

"Sometimes you question yourself. But sometimes you have to lean on the people around you. They were nothing but supportive. When you have a group that's as close as ours is — the hard times are hard, but you can have those hard and honest conversations with each other and we did that when things weren't going well."

Things went well Tuesday. With rare exception, the Blues were in control against a San Jose team missing three injured mainstays: Erik Karlsson, Joe Pavelski and Tomas Hertl.

The team that scored first won every game in this series, and on Tuesday it was David Perron on a tip-in of a Sammy Blais shot just 92 seconds into play.

"I've never played in an atmosphere like that," Blais said. "I think it was incredible at the end when they were singing, 'We want the Cup!' Everyone on the bench had chills and it was a great moment."

Blues players celebrate Tyler Bozak's goal — the fourth for the Blues — during the third period of the historic Game 6 victory.